MW00395907

# SIMPLE FRENCH PALEO

### FLAVORFUL ALLERGEN-FREE RECIPES
### FOR THE AUTOIMMUNE PROTOCOL

*Sophie Van Tiggelen*

#### FOUNDER OF A SQUIRREL IN THE KITCHEN

*Copyright © 2016 Sophie Van Tiggelen*
www.asquirrelinthekitchen.com

All rights reserved. No part of this publication may be reproduced or distributed in any form or by any means, electronic or mechanical, or stored in a database or retrieval system, without prior written permission from the author.

*ISBN:* 978-1-53333-160-1

*Written and photographed by* Sophie Van Tiggelen
*Cover and interior design by* Chelsey Luther
*Watercolor illustration page 32 by* Diane Van Tiggelen
*Map credit by* Free Vector Maps

*\* DISCLAIMER: The content presented in this book is for entertainment purposes only. The purchaser of this book understands that the author is not a medical professional, and the information contained within this book is not intended to replace medical advice or meant to be relied upon to treat, cure, or prevent any disease, illness, or medical condition. It is understood that you will seek full medical clearance by a licensed physician before making any changes mentioned in this book. The author claims no responsibility to any person or entity for any liability, loss, or damage caused or alleged to be caused directly or indirectly as a result of the use, application, or interpretation of the material in this book.*

# Table of Contents

## FOREWORD

*In the past, an autoimmune diagnosis meant you had few options besides the conventional treatments, which at best, aim at symptom management (if you're lucky!) and not disease reversal or true healing. Today, we are lucky to live in a new reality as far as the diagnosis, treatment, and management of autoimmune disease is concerned. If you find yourself here, you can now combine natural, approachable dietary and lifestyle interventions as well as other tools from the worlds of functional medicine, naturopathy, and other healing modalities with what is available in conventional medicine (or, avoid it altogether!). If you have an autoimmune disease you can take steps to live better despite chronic illness, and the contents of this book will help you do just that!*

I'm no stranger to healing from these conditions, having been diagnosed with Hashimoto's and celiac disease in my mid-twenties and experiencing an extreme health crisis as a result. Hitting "rock bottom" motivated me to learn everything I could about the connection between diet, lifestyle, and autoimmune disease, since conventional medicine left me with few options for a better life. In short, I had to figure out how to heal my body, because nobody was going to do it for me!

After turning my health around with *The Autoimmune Protocol*, a variation of the Paleo diet aimed at eliminating food allergies and sensitivities, restoring nutrient status, and balancing gut flora, I went back to school to become a Nutritional Therapy Practitioner. While at first I imagined using this education to inform my work as a personal chef, I ended up starting *Autoimmune-Paleo. com*, and writing *The Autoimmune Paleo Cookbook*, both resources aimed at enabling those with chronic illness to heal their bodies with dietary and lifestyle changes. The rest, as they say, is history, as thousands of people began to change their lives using these natural approaches, and the AIP movement was born!

I was connected to Sophie in the early days of the AIP blogging community and became instantly attracted to her unique style of cooking and beautiful photography, not to mention our common Hashimoto's diagnosis. Her warmth and enthusiasm radiated through those entries on her blog and we quickly sparked a friendship. She offered to host me while I was passing through Colorado on a book tour, and I was treated to a little slice of AIP heaven that week... I left having been nourished both by the incredible food she so lovingly shared as well as the friendship and conversation that we had.

While Sophie's cooking is deeply rooted in tradition and family history, it has all of the elements that I love—simple, practical, flavorful, and fresh. Being a fairly restricted diet, The Autoimmune Protocol can sometimes get a bit boring and mundane, and Simple French Paleo serves to be a unique resource for anyone who is looking to infuse some new flavors and combinations into their routine. You may think that good cooking takes a lot of fancy equipment or time, but the recipes contained here will show you otherwise. Most can easily be prepared in 40 minutes or less, with only one pot, making them the perfect answer to the question, "What's for dinner?" Try the Niçoise Salad (p.84), the Country-Style Chicken Soup (p.116), or the Meatballs with Nomato Sauce (p.168)—you won't be disappointed!

One of the biggest lessons I've learned from Sophie is the art of enjoying food. Often on the elimination diet, our meals can become a product of necessity, driven by nutrient status and the basic task of feeding ourselves. Taking the time to sit down and enjoy a meal is actually a factor in promoting optimal digestion, as our bodies assimilate food best when we are in a relaxed state, chewing well, and in the company of others. These recipes make it easy, as your family and friends will all be strategizing how to invite themselves over for dinner after they've discovered the delicious turn your cooking adventures have taken!

I urge you, as you flip through the pages of this book and mark the recipes that are sure to become family favorites, to not only look to the task of feeding yourself, but of nourishing your spirit and creativity with these incredible recipes Sophie has created. Embarking on the Autoimmune Protocol has never been so enjoyable!

—Mickey Trescott, NTP, author of *The Autoimmune Paleo Cookbook* and co-author of *The Autoimmune Wellness Handbook*

*I have always loved Provence.*
*In Belgium, where I was raised, we were highly influenced by French culture and food, but for me, the region of Provence had a particular draw. It is a landscape of green, blue, yellow, and purple. Of olive groves, wild herbs, tall grasses, and miles and miles of lavender fields. The air is rich with the warmth of the sun and if you stop long enough, you can hear the soft, soothing song of cicadas.*

My Provence is peppered with stone houses covered in generations of wild flowers and ivy, church bells calling the hour, and narrow lanes revealing treasures to those who seek them. Bustling alfresco markets and cafés play host to those who wish only to eat, drink, and enjoy the bounty and beauty of life.

It sounds quite wonderful, doesn't it? And to think, I haven't even mentioned the food yet!

*Provençal cuisine is simple and fresh.* It doesn't rely on exotic ingredients, rather it strives to preserve the natural flavors of the fresh fruits, vegetables, meats and fish found easily at stores and farmer's markets. It is a natural fit for those adopting the Paleo Autoimmune Protocol. I know many people believe that French cuisine is overly elaborate and difficult to prepare, but the reality of everyday French food differs greatly from what you would find in a lavish French restaurant. You may be surprised to learn how simple, healthy, and homey true traditional French fare is. This is especially the case with the foods of Provence.

Imagine a roast chicken, skin golden and crisp. Now picture a large casserole of ratatouille, vibrant and fragrant with herbs. A delicate pear cake rests on the counter, waiting patiently to help you finish your meal. Do you prefer fish? We can easily prepare a whole fish instead, baked slowly to perfection in the oven, and serve it with a fresh, crisp salad and a bowl of tangy, celeriac remoulade. Perhaps bouillabaisse, brandade, Niçoise salad, herbed roast lamb, French onion soup, stuffed mushrooms,

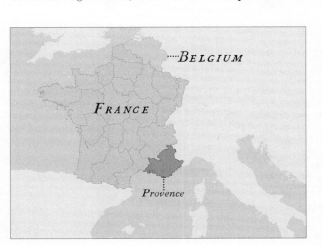

BELGIUM

FRANCE

Provence

pâté, marinated olives, tapenade, crèpes, or chocolate mousse sound better? What suits your fancy?

By now, I hope you have come to understand that I believe eating for your health does not have to mean bland, tedious meals. Deciding to take your health into your own hands is a momentous decision and is not without its challenges. In 2009, I developed Hashimoto's disease. It was during this time of upheaval that I adopted the Paleo Autoimmune Protocol. I was desperate to feel healthy and get back to the business of living. And living well! I was not interested in half a life. I found myself making radical changes to the way I ate and to be honest, it was difficult. I could no longer just grab anything off a shelf and be safe. I read labels and thought very carefully about what I was putting into my body. Would it cause me pain? Would my inflammation sky-rocket because of one tiny little ingredient I could not pronounce? The world of eating was no longer simple, and I longed for simple.

My struggle led me back to the traditional French cooking of my youth and I rediscovered how simple and honest food could be. I was reminded that fresh, real food is at the heart of life and that even as I struggled with an auto-immune condition, I could still enjoy the pleasures life had to offer.

With this book, I hope to remind you of the same thing. These pages contain a wealth of soul-soothing food. Each and every recipe is compliant with the elimination phase of the Paleo Autoimmune Protocol as described by Sarah Ballantyne in her phenomenal book, The Paleo Approach. In addition to the recipes, I have included details about my own story, about the Paleo Auto-immune Protocol (also referred to as AIP) and how to incorporate its tenants into your life, and tips on how to create an AIP kitchen. It is my hope that this book will help you on your journey toward true health and a full, rich life. Of course, I'm also very excited to share so many delicious French recipes with you. I hope you find them as nourishing and enjoyable as I do.

*Bon appétit!*

*Layered Raspberry Crèpe Cake, page 196*

THE FIRST SYMPTOMS OF MY AUTOIMMUNE disease were rather brutal. After a minor outpatient surgery in early 2009, I woke up in the middle of the night in the grip of a full-blown panic attack. Fully alert and totally disoriented, my heart was pounding out of my chest, my breathing was shallow and fast, and my hands and legs were alive with a terrible tingling sensation. I thought I was having a heart attack. I came to understand that I was not, but the experience was frightening to say the least.

After that first episode, I suffered from anxiety and panic attacks on a daily basis for months. I never knew when an attack would strike and soon even the idea of having to face one at all became worse than the attack itself. I developed severe insomnia and if you have ever had insomnia, you know what a torment it is to lie awake hour after hour, utterly exhausted, yet unable to fall asleep. Several times, my panic attacks landed me in the local emergency room. Ultimately, I was prescribed anti-anxiety medication. Desperate, I took them grudgingly, and in truth, the medication did help reduce my anxiety, but it didn't treat the cause of my panic disorder.

## — A Downward Spiral —

Months into my ordeal, I noticed that my thyroid (a butterfly-shaped gland at the base of the throat that regulates metabolism, among other things) was swollen and painful. It felt like a tennis ball was stuck in my throat, which, as you can imagine, was very uncomfortable and made it difficult to swallow. I was also experiencing a string of unsettling symptoms: anxiety, insomnia, heart palpitations, dizziness, brain fog, cognitive impairment, aches and pains all over my body, bloating, constipation, hair loss, dry and itchy skin, and mucus over-production. The medications prescribed to me seemed to have no effect and no one could say what was wrong with me.

## ⟶ *I Could No Longer Function* ⟶

At my lowest point, and still suffering from incapacitating insomnia, I was unable to work. Basic household tasks—grocery shopping, preparing meals, caring for my children—all became impossible. I was exhausted all the time. What little energy I had left was dedicated to consulting with doctors and subjecting myself to an ongoing battery of laboratory tests. I kept changing doctors hoping the next one might finally figure out what ailed me. Needless to say, this put an enormous strain on my family, both financially and emotionally.

## ⟶ *Surely, This Can't Be It* ⟶

I asked myself that question everyday. "Surely, this can't be how I am going to spend the rest of my life. Surely not." That's when I started working with a functional medicine practitioner and true healing began. He helped me look at the bigger picture and implement changes that would ultimately bring me back to health. I stopped taking all my anti-anxiety medications and approached my healing in a more natural and holistic way. In-depth testing of my thyroid revealed the presence of antibodies attacking the gland. I was diagnosed with Hashimoto's Thyroiditis, was prescribed natural thyroid hormone replacement, and adopted a gluten-free diet. Finally, with a firm diagnosis and a plan, I looked forward to being healthy once again.

## ⟶ *Not Quite Enough* ⟶

With the help of my new thyroid medication, I was able to slowly overcome my panic attacks. The relief I felt was tremendous, however, the rest of my symptoms lingered and my overall health continued to deteriorate until, in 2012, I began experiencing excruciating joint pain. The pain was so intense that I couldn't walk. I was desperate to find a way to "fix" myself.

I began spending a lot of time conducting online research and stumbled upon the Paleo Autoimmune Protocol (also referred to as AIP). I read stories from people who had successfully reversed their autoimmune disease through diet and lifestyle modification and so, with absolutely nothing to lose, I decided to give AIP a go!

I dove headfirst into the elimination phase of the Paleo Autoimmune Protocol and eliminated all listed trigger foods at once (*see page* 33–34 for a list of foods to avoid during the elimination phase). Going cold turkey worked for me—severe pain is a great motivator!

Once I began AIP, I experienced rapid improvement of my worst symptoms, specifically the joint pain and anxiety, however, I didn't feel the legendary "energy boost" so many people report when starting this diet. Even though I was following AIP to the letter, I continued to struggle for several months with intense fatigue and sluggishness. With time and patience however, my autoimmune flares became less frequent, less intense, and I recovered from them more quickly. My head cleared, I began sleeping better, and I slowly regained my energy.

## The Importance of Support

Since the very beginning of my healing journey, I have been very fortunate to have the unconditional love and support of my husband and children. Their open-minded attitudes and encouragement have been instrumental in my continued faithfulness to the Paleo Autoimmune Protocol. After a short transition period, during which time I found my bearings with my new lifestyle, my family began following the protocol with me. What a tremendous gift that was! I began developing tasty AIP-based meals that were nutritious and satisfying enough even for those not suffering from an autoimmune disorder. I have even been able to convert some of my children's favorite meals into AIP-friendly versions built around a wide variety of vegetables, meats, and seafood. It is my hope that sharing these recipes might aid in your recovery and also delight you and your family, as they have mine.

## Commitment Matters

My commitment to the Paleo Autoimmune Protocol allowed me to put my autoimmune disease into remission. This doesn't mean that once I started

feeling better I began eating the way I used to! I still have to watch what I eat and avoid inflammatory foods, but I have been able to relax a little and reintroduce a few foods I had eliminated at the beginning.

The anti-inflammatory benefits of the Paleo Autoimmune Protocol have had far reaching and positive influences in my life. I am healthy again. I am stronger and fitter than I was ten years ago. Most importantly, I now have a positive outlook on life and look forward to the future with joy and anticipation.

I wish this for you, too.

THE PALEO AUTOIMMUNE PROTOCOL (ALSO REferred to as AIP) is a specific version of the Paleo diet with special adaptations made to address autoimmune conditions. *It is a powerful healing tool designed to reduce chronic inflammation in the body, restore a healthy digestive tract, and regulate the immune system.*

Your body has an amazing ability to heal itself when given the proper resources and the opportunity to do so. The basic principles of the Paleo Autoimmune Protocol rest on that theory. AIP stresses that by eating a real food diet and focusing on nutrient density, you can set the stage for healing to occur and reverse the effects of autoimmune disease.

In her book "The Paleo Approach: Reverse Autoimmune Disease and Heal Your Body," Sarah Ballantyne explains the mechanism of autoimmune disease. I recommend her book if you wish to delve deeper into the scientific aspects of autoimmunity and AIP.

In a nutshell, autoimmune disease is caused by the immune system mistakenly attacking your own body and organs rather than protecting them. For example, in the case of Hashimoto's Thyroiditis, the immune system attacks the thyroid.

The presence of gut dysbiosis (having the wrong kind or wrong number of bacteria in the gut) and a leaky gut (increased intestinal permeability) are almost always involved with autoimmune disease. The good news is we can help our gut and regulate our immune system with an appropriate diet and a few basic lifestyle changes.

The Paleo Autoimmune Protocol can be divided into 3 phases:
1. **the elimination phase,**
2. **the reintroduction phase,** *AND*
3. **the maintenance phase.**

→ *One* ←

# THE ELIMINATION PHASE

The elimination phase contains a double-edged approach:

1) **Remove all potential trigger foods** that create chronic harmful inflammation and irritate the gut.

2) **Add nutrient-dense foods** to provide the body with the building blocks needed to repair and heal the gut.

*REMOVING INFLAMMATORY FOODS* **+** *ADDING NUTRIENT-DENSE FOODS* **=** *HEALING*

## — Eliminate Inflammatory Foods —

There are several reasons why we eliminate inflammatory foods on the Paleo Autoimmune Protocol. They provide little nutrition (but a lot of calories), are difficult to digest, compromise gut microbiome, contribute to hormone dysregulation, and increase inflammation in the body.

Any and all of these things can trigger an autoimmune response. For this reason, it is best to remove all trigger foods until you can figure out your own food allergies and sensitivities. Think of the elimination phase as a reset button for your body. This is the time in which deep healing can happen.

This seems like a good opportunity to talk about the temporary nature of the elimination phase. This phase of restricted eating is not meant to last forever. It is meant to be a time of calming, a time of healing. Nearly everyone embarking on this journey will require a minimum of 30 days in the elimination phase, some will require longer, but no one will need to remain there forever. A restricted life is not the goal—health is.

## — *The Plan* —

The elimination phase of AIP requires you to eliminate many foods that are already restricted on a standard Paleo diet including grains (and gluten), dried legumes (including soy and peanuts), food chemicals and additives, and refined and processed foods.

In addition to this, there are further problematic foods to avoid on the Paleo Autoimmune Protocol including dairy, eggs, nightshades, nuts and seeds (including coffee and cocoa), fresh legumes (green beans, green peas), and alcohol. (*See table on page 33–34 for a complete list of foods to avoid.*)

Some people embrace AIP and eliminate these inflammatory foods all at once. Others prefer a more progressive approach. A good example of a more progressive method is the online coaching program developed by Angie Alt called "SAD to AIP in SIX". The basic principle of her program is to remove one group of problematic foods per week, for 6 weeks, ending up on a strict AIP elimination phase diet.

Whether you dive in headfirst or slowly dip your toes in, your commitment to the Paleo Autoimmune Protocol is paramount. There is no 70/30 or 80/20 on AIP. You need to commit fully to this healing phase in order to see improvements.

## — *Add Nutrient-Dense Foods* —

Please don't be alarmed by the foods you need to eliminate when beginning AIP. There are still plenty of wholesome, health-promoting, delicious foods you can eat! There is literally a bounty of health-promoting foods available to you!

If you are suffering from an autoimmune disease, chances are you have nutrient deficiencies. Nutrients such as vitamins and minerals are essential for good health, which is why you will focus on eating the most nutrient-dense foods you can find while on the protocol.

I know it sounds daunting, but believe me, you won't have to sacrifice flavor or variety in order to heal. In fact, the recipes in this cookbook will show you how to prepare delicious meals that you and your family will love—even crave!

These delicious, nutrient-dense foods include: grass-fed meats, organ meats, wild-caught seafood, a wide variety of both green and colorful vegetables, fruit, healthy fats, fermented foods, and bone broth.

AIP isn't about finding rare, exotic ingredients. It is about going back to the basics—to simple, real ingredients that will promote health instead of creating inflammation. In truth, the Paleo Autoimmune Protocol is a very simple, healing diet that you will truly relish. (*See table on page 35–37 for a complete list of foods to include and a list of foods to eat in moderation.*)

## — Guidelines for a Happy Gut —

* Eat between 8 to 14 cups of vegetables per day (measured raw)
* Eat a wide variety of colorful fruit and vegetables
* Choose seasonal fruits and vegetables
* Choose organic grass-fed meats, organ meats, and wild-caught seafood (budget permitting)
* Consume healthy fats at every meal
* Consume fermented foods and drinks
* Consume bone broth

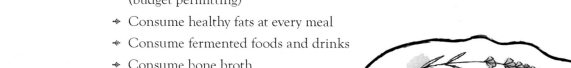

## MY IDEAL AIP PLATE

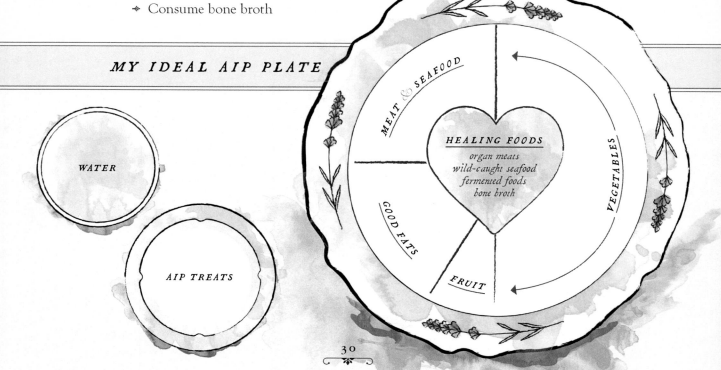

WATER

AIP TREATS

MEAT & SEAFOOD

VEGETABLES

GOOD FATS

FRUIT

HEALING FOODS

*organ meats*
*wild-caught seafood*
*fermented foods*
*bone broth*

## ⎯ Notes on Fruit and AIP Treats ⎯

Fruit is a great source of fiber, vitamins, minerals, and antioxidants, however, while in the elimination phase of AIP it is preferable to keep your daily consumption to between one and three servings per day (about 20 grams of fructose). If you love fruit and feel this may be difficult, think about it in terms of choices. For example, one medium apple has around six grams of fructose while one cup of raspberries has just over two grams of fructose. In general, fresh berries are always a good choice as they have a lower fructose content than other fruit.

Note that dried fruit has a very high glycemic load and should be avoided or eaten sparingly!

Why? Sugar is always sugar, even when it comes from fruit or unprocessed natural sweeteners like honey and maple syrup. In my experience, too much sugar doesn't mix well with autoimmune disease. Sugar can raise overall inflammation in your body and make autoimmune symptoms worse.

Sweets and desserts made with ingredients compliant with the Paleo Autoimmune Protocol are wonderful and special, but we should treat them as such. A little something sweet to celebrate a special occasion is a wonderful treat, not an everyday occurrence.

## ⎯ Notes on Healthy Fats ⎯

You might be surprised by the important role healthy fats play in the Paleo Autoimmune Protocol. After all, we have been bombarded with scientific literature pointing the finger at all fats as being the culprit for heart disease. It turns out that the long-established dietary recommendation to avoid fat was wrong, leading to grave vitamin deficiencies. In fact, our bodies need healthy fats to function properly. Healthy fats are a fundamental component of our hormones and we need them to properly absorb many fat-soluble vitamins and nutrients.

Plus, it tastes good!

Some examples of recommended healthy fats are avocados (and avocado oil), fatty fish (sardines, mackerel, wild salmon), grass-fed animal products (including lard and tallow), extra-virgin olive oil, coconut oil and coconut butter, and palm oil.

Try to eat healthy fats at every meal. For example, an avocado sprinkled with sea salt or canned sardines in olive oil both make terrific mid-afternoon snacks. Don't tell me there isn't anything to eat on AIP!

## ⋙ FOODS TO AVOID ⋘

### Grains

| | | |
|---|---|---|
| amaranth | kamut | sorghum |
| barley | millet | spelt |
| buckwheat | oats | teff |
| bulgur | quinoa | wheat |
| corn | rice | |
| farro | rye | |

### Beans & Legumes

| | | |
|---|---|---|
| adzuki beans | Great Northern beans | peas |
| black beans | green beans | pinto beans |
| black-eyed peas | kidney beans | split peas |
| calico beans | lentils | red beans |
| cannellini beans | lima beans | soybeans |
| chickpeas | navy beans | sugar snap peas |
| fava beans | peanuts | white beans |

### Nightshades

| | | |
|---|---|---|
| ashwagandha | ground cherries | tomatoes |
| hell peppers | hot peppers | tomatillos |
| eggplant | potatoes | *Also see spices derived from nightshades |
| goji berries | tobacco | |

### Other

| | | |
|---|---|---|
| alcohol | processed sugars | |
| emulsifiers | processed vegetable oils | NSAID medications (check with doctor for pain management) |
| food additives | sugar substitutes (including stevia) | |
| food chemicals | thickeners | |

# Eggs

| chicken eggs | duck eggs | goose eggs | quail eggs |

# Dairy

| butter | cream cheese | kefir |
| buttermilk | frozen yogurt | milk |
| butter oil | goat cheese | sour cream |
| cheese | goat milk | whey |
| cottage cheese | ice cream | whey protein |
| cream | ghee | yogurt |

# Nuts & Seeds

| almond | flax | poppy |
| Brazil nut | hazelnut | pumpkin |
| cashew | hemp | sesame |
| chestnut | macadamia | sunflower |
| chia | pecan | |
| cocoa | pine nut | *Including flours, butters, and oils derived from nuts & seeds* |
| coffee | pistachio | |

# Herbs & Spices

| allspice | cumin | pepper (all kinds) |
| anise seed | curry | poppy seed |
| caraway | dill seed | red pepper * |
| cardamom | fennel seed | sesame seed |
| cayenne pepper * | fenugreek | star anise |
| celery seed | juniper | sumac |
| chili pepper flakes * | mustard seed | whole vanilla bean |
| chili powder * | nutmeg | |
| coriander seed | paprika * | *Spices derived from nightshades* |

## FOODS TO INCLUDE

### Vegetables

| | | |
|---|---|---|
| artichoke | cucumber | radish |
| arugula | dandelion | radicchio |
| asparagus | endive | rhubarb |
| beet | fennel | rutabaga |
| bok choy | jicama | shallot |
| broccoli | kale | spinach |
| Brussels sprouts | kohlrabi | summer squash |
| butternut squash | leek | sweet potato |
| cabbage | lettuce | taro |
| carrot | mushroom | turnip |
| cauliflower | mustard greens | watercress |
| celeriac | napa cabbage | winter squash |
| celery | onion | yam |
| chard | parsnip | yuca |
| collard greens | pumpkin | zucchini |

### Herbs & Spices

| | | |
|---|---|---|
| basil leaf | ginger | sage |
| bay leaf | lavender | savory |
| chamomile | lemongrass | sea salt |
| chives | mace | tarragon |
| cilantro | marjoram | thyme |
| cinnamon | mint | turmeric |
| cloves | oregano leaf | vanilla extract (if cooked or baked) and vanilla powder |
| dill weed | parsley | |
| fennel leaf | rosemary | |
| garlic | saffron | |

# *Fruits*

| | | |
|---|---|---|
| apple | fig | papaya |
| apricot | grape | peach |
| avocado | grapefruit | pear |
| banana | guava | persimmon |
| blackberry | huckleberry | plantain |
| blueberry | honeydew | plum |
| cantaloupe | kiwi | pineapple |
| cherry | lemon | pomegranate |
| clementine | lime | raspberry |
| coconut | mango | strawberry |
| cranberry | nectarine | tangerine |
| date | orange | watermelon |

# *Proteins*

| *MEATS* | *FISH* | *SHELLFISH* | *ORGAN MEATS* |
|---|---|---|---|
| beef | anchovies | clams | bone broth |
| bison | catfish | crab | gizzard |
| chicken | cod | crawfish | heart |
| duck | halibut | lobster | kidney |
| elk | herring | mussels | liver |
| lamb | mackerel | octopus | tongue |
| mutton | mahi mahi | oysters | |
| pork | salmon | prawns | |
| rabbit | sardines | scallops | |
| turkey | snapper | shrimp | |
| venison | tilapia | squid | |
| yak | trout | | |
| | tuna | | |

## Ferments

| fermented vegetables | kombucha | sauerkraut | water kefir |
|---|---|---|---|

## Fats

| animal fat | duck fat | palm oil |
|---|---|---|
| avocado oil | lard | tallow |
| coconut oil | olive oil | |

## Sweeteners

| dates | honey | molasses |
|---|---|---|
| dried fruits | maple syrup | |

## Pantry Items

*See page 49*

---

### ⋆ FOODS TO CONSUME IN MODERATION ⋆

| | | |
|---|---|---|
| green and black tea | AIP treats and baked goods | moderate to high gylcemic load fruits and vegetables |
| fructose (10–20 grams per day) | coconut products | |
| salt (use mineral rich salts) | natural sweeteners | |

## ⇨ *Two* ⇦

# THE REINTRODUCTION PHASE

As I mentioned, the elimination phase of the Paleo Autoimmune Protocol is not meant to last forever. It is a temporary time of healing. The next part, the reintroduction phase, is the fun part. This is where you get to bring foods back into your daily diet that you had previously eliminated and you get to begin to truly understand your body—a win-win!

Please note that this doesn't mean that you will go back to the way you were eating before AIP. All the foods creating gut inflammation, leaky gut, and stimulating the immune system are still off limits, but this is the time when you will start to understand what that means for your long-term diet.

The goal is to progressively reintroduce foods and get you on a diet that more closely resembles a standard paleo or primal diet. The final result of the reintroduction process is different for everyone and will depend on your own food sensibilities.

## — *When Can I Start?* —

As mentioned, everyone will require a minimum of 30 days in the elimination phase, although it is better to wait three to four months. Some people, often those who are severely ill and require a great deal of healing, wait a full year. The longer you wait, the better chance your body has to heal and prepare for new foods. Resist the temptation to rush the reintroductions to satisfy your cravings. Take the time to heal. It will be worth the wait!

If you are still suffering from autoimmune flares, digestive distress, or chronic pain, it is definitely too soon. ***Wait until you see a significant improvement in your symptoms and your gut has healed before attempting any reintroduction.***

It is also important to make sure that all other important aspects of your life are well managed including stress levels, sleep, and exercise. Good health involves far more than the food we eat. AIP, while primarily concerned with food, incorporates all aspects of life.

The bottom line is—there isn't a hard and fast rule to determine the best time to start reintroductions. Ideally, AIP will help you learn to read the signals your body is sending you. Listen to those signals and exercise your own good judgment. You will know when the time is right.

## — *How Do I Reintroduce Foods?* —

The basic procedure for reintroducing foods involves eating the chosen new food several times throughout the day and monitoring your body for symptoms. Introduce new foods one at a time and do not rush.

(If you notice symptoms at any time during the process, stop eating the newly introduced food immediately and try again after your symptoms resolve completely.)

1. Choose **one** food to reintroduce.
2. Eat one half teaspoon and wait for 15 minutes.
3. If no symptoms appear, eat one teaspoon and wait for another 15 minutes.
4. If no symptoms appear, eat one and one half teaspoons and wait two to three hours.
5. If you still have no reaction, eat a normal-size portion, then wait three days before eating it again.

Monitor yourself closely for symptoms. A reaction will usually appear within one to four hours after eating the food, but may take up to three days.

Symptoms will vary from person to person and can be either mild or acute. They usually will exacerbate your autoimmune disease symptoms. Symptoms can include digestive troubles, mood swings, reduced energy, unusual food cravings, sleep disturbances, hives, headaches, skin reaction, joint pain, and brain fog, among others.

In her book "Reintroducing Foods on the Paleo Autoimmune Protocol," Eileen Laird talks about a "*second phase in the reintroduction process.*" Laird suggests that after you have successfully completed the five first steps, a sixth step should be undertaken. She suggests eating the new food in small quantities every day for another week. The reason for this added precaution is that not all food reactions are strong or immediate. Some reactions are the result of a cumulative effect that becomes noticeable only after repeated consumption. If, after this extra step, you still feel good, you are in the clear!

## — *In What Order Do I Reintroduce Foods?* —

In her book "The Paleo Approach: Reverse Autoimmune Disease and Heal your Body," Sarah Ballantyne lays out a template for the order of reintroductions. The guide is divided into four stages, giving priority to the most nutrient-dense foods which are least likely to create a reaction. I encourage you to seek out Sarah Ballantyne's website (thepaleomom.com) or her book for any questions you may have.

## FOUR PHASES OF REINTRODUCTIONS

### Phase 1

*EGG YOLKS*
preferably from soy-free chicken

*FRESH LEGUMES WITH EDIBLE PODS*
green beans, peas, sugar snap pea, etc

*FRUIT-BASED SPICES*
allspice, cardamom, juniper, pepper, vanilla bean

*SEED-BASED SPICES*
anise, caraway, celery seed, coriander, cumin, fennel, mustard, nutmeg, etc

*SEED AND NUT OILS*
sesame, macadamia, and walnut oil

*GRASS-FED GHEE*

### Phase 2

*SEEDS*
whole, ground, and butters

*NUTS*
whole, ground, and butter (except cashews and pistachios)

*COCOA AND CHOCOLATE*

*EGG WHITES*
preferably from soy-free chicken

*GRASS-FED BUTTER*
sesame, macadamia, and walnut oil

*ALCOHOL IN SMALL QUANTITIES*

## NOTES ON REINTRODUCTIONS:

✦ You may be able to tolerate some foods only in small quantities, and even then only occasionally. This is the case for me with coffee and chocolate. I enjoy them as a special treat now and then.

✦ Keeping a food journal to track the foods you reintroduce and your reactions will make the process easier. It will help you identify patterns and links between foods and symptoms.

✦ Quantities when reintroducing spices are much smaller than for other foods like nuts or egg whites. A good approach is to prepare a dish that you would season heavily with the spice you wish to test. Then follow the steps outlined previously, starting with a small bite, then two bites, then three, then a whole portion of the dish.

# Phase 3

CASHEWS AND PISTACHIOS

EGGPLANT

SWEET BELL PEPPERS

PAPRIKA

COFFEE

GRASS-FED CREAM

GRASS-FED FERMENTED DAIRY
yogurt, kefir

# Phase 4

OTHER GRASS-FED DAIRY PRODUCTS
whole milk, cheese

OTHER NIGHTSHADES AND NIGHTSHADE SPICES
including chili peppers, tomatoes, potatoes

ALCOHOL IN LARGER QUANTITIES

WHITE RICE*

SOAKED AND FERMENTED DRIED LEGUMES*
sesame, macadamia, and walnut oil

SOAKED AND FERMENTED GLUTEN-FREE GRAINS*

> \* *These foods are not part of the standard Paleo diet. However, some people who have achieved full remission of their autoimmune disease choose to reintroduce these foods into their diet. Only you can decide which way to go, based on how you feel.*

⤙ The reintroduction process for alcoholic beverages differs from other foods. To begin, drink only one small glass of gluten-free alcohol. If no symptoms appear, wait at least one week before having another glass. If the reintroduction is successful, limit your consumption to a maximum of two glasses of alcohol per week.

*ONE SMALL GLASS =*

    8–9 ounces gluten-free beer or cider

    5 ounces wine

    3–4 ounces fortified wine

    2–3 ounces liquor

    1–1½ ounces spirits

→ *Three* ←

# THE MAINTENANCE PHASE

The process of the reintroduction phase of the Paleo Autoimmune Protocol (also referred to as AIP) will help you discover which foods benefit your body and which foods trigger inflammation and autoimmune flares. The maintenance phase is where you hold it all together.

At this point, your diet will most likely look like a cross between strict AIP and a standard paleo/primal diet. This will be your maintenance diet, or "personalized AIP" as Eileen Laird calls it in her "Simple Guide to the Paleo Autoimmune Protocol." You are a unique snowflake and your diet will reflect that from here on out!

Know that the foods you tolerate may vary over time. A food that you have reintroduced successfully in the past might become problematic again in the future, especially if your "balance" is compromised (increased stress, poor sleep, infections, etc.). For this reason, it is important to be vigilant and keep an eye out for sneaky, slow-moving symptoms. Be ready to exclude any trigger foods from your diet should you notice any symptoms creeping in—at least for a while.

As a general rule, anytime you experience a resurgence of old autoimmune symptoms or the presentation of new ones, it is a good idea to retreat to the elimination phase for a period, until your symptoms have completely resolved.

As you get on with your life and start to experiment with new foods, keep the basic principles of the Paleo Autoimmune Protocol top of mind:

- ❧ prioritize nutrient density,
- ❧ eat a wide variety of health-promoting foods, *AND*
- ❧ keep your gut healthy.

It is important for you to find your own balance. Consider what makes you happy—body, mind, and soul—and build your new healthy life around that balanced approach.

## A WORD ABOUT LIFESTYLE

*A*N EXPLANATION OF THE *PALEO AUTO*-immune Protocol would not be complete if I didn't mention the importance of the lifestyle choices you will need to make. Healing from an autoimmune disease is not just about food. While the food you eat (and don't eat) is extremely important in reducing systemic inflammation and allowing your body to heal, other factors are also at play.

## — Reduce Emotional Stress —

Keeping your stress level as low as possible is paramount when dealing with an autoimmune disease. In fact, too much stress can completely derail your best efforts with your diet. Chronic stress increases systemic inflammation and can worsen the symptoms of autoimmune disease. Not fun!

The good news is there are many ways you can reduce stress in your life. Meditation is, of course, an obvious choice, but there are many other techniques available to help you reduce stress that don't require a mantra or chanting. Guided relaxation, yoga, mindful stretching, time spent outdoors, massage, adult coloring, warm baths, listening to music, the possibilities are truly endless.

## — Cultivate Sleep —

This one is dear to my heart. I suffered greatly from insomnia at the onset of my autoimmune disease and I know intimately the toll it can take on the mind and body. Inadequate sleep increases inflammation and makes it harder for your body to deal with stress and pain. *For true, restful sleep, aim for seven to nine hours of sleep every night.*

As with stress reduction, there are many techniques that can aid a good night's sleep. Here are a few I found helpful when overcoming my insomnia.

- Go for a gentle walk to get some fresh air and sunlight.
- Practice regular relaxation techniques to quiet racing thoughts and lower anxiety.
- Develop a bedtime routine to wind down at the end of the day.
- Keep overly stimulating activities for mornings.
- Eat a balanced and nutritious meal at least two hours before bedtime.
- Avoid sugary foods and drinks.
- Prioritize calming activities in the evening like taking a warm bath with lavender salts, reading an enjoyable book, gentle stretches, listening to soft music.
- Make sure your bedroom is comfortable and inviting; keep it cool, dark, and quiet.

## ⟶ *Practice Regular Exercise* ⟵

Everybody knows that exercise has a beneficial impact on health. We were designed to stand, move, gather, and hunt after all! Exercise will boost your immune system, increase your mood, and help you sleep better.

That being said, at one point during my illness just getting out of the house for a short walk was the biggest accomplishment of my day! The important thing is that you keep moving. There's no need to train for a marathon, in fact, exercise that is too strenuous can cause physical exhaustion and trigger an autoimmune flare, so take it easy, but be sure to *move*.

The key is to start slowly and listen to your body. Begin with gentle activities like walking, restorative yoga, or swimming, for example. Once you get your energy back and feel stronger, you can then step up your exercise routine. I would, however, recommend that you keep it low-impact if you have sensitive joints.

## ⟶ *Remain Hopeful* ⟵

What we think and how we feel impacts our immune system. We are complex creatures and our minds and bodies are connected. Have you ever experienced a tightening in your stomach before an important event? Or perhaps trembling fingers and shortness of breath after a frightening incident? You see? That's the mind-body connection. Our thoughts have the power to induce a physical reaction in our body. Entertaining negative thoughts toward yourself or losing faith in the future is common when dealing with an autoimmune disease, but it will not help you heal.

Try instead to be gentle with yourself. Give your inner voice permission to speak to you the way you would to a suffering loved one. Remind yourself that others are walking the same path you are walking at this moment. You are not alone.

Remember that many people, including myself, have seen tremendous improvements in their lives thanks to the Paleo Autoimmune Protocol, from a reduction of symptoms to complete remission! If I can do it, so can you!

Remain hopeful and focus on achieving a positive end result. It *will* help.

AIL DE PAYS
8€kg

*I* KNOW THAT DIVING INTO AIP CAN SEEM DAUNT-ing, especially when you have never even heard of some of the ingredients needed to create some of these recipes! You may be wondering what your pantry should look like now that you have decided to change your life and make no mistake—a well-stocked pantry *will* make your new life easier.

In order to help you get organized, I have compiled a list of my AIP pantry staples. All of the listed ingredients are compliant with the Paleo Autoimmune Protocol. I use them on a daily basis to prepare food for my family and myself. Along with lots of fresh vegetables, fruit, meat, and seafood, these items represent the core of my diet. It is a relatively brief list, which means you should be able to build yourself a well-stocked AIP pantry quickly. I find most of these items at my local health food store, however, if you are unable to locate an item in person, there is always Amazon or Thrive Market.

**As a general rule, always read labels carefully and avoid additives, preservatives, chemicals, and added sugar.**

## My AIP Pantry Staples

- *APPLE CIDER VINEGAR:* I often use apple cider vinegar in salad dressings and marinades for its fresh and zesty flavor. My preferred brand is *Bragg*, which is organic, raw, unfiltered, and unpasteurized.

- *ARROWROOT STARCH:* Also known as arrowroot flour, I use arrowroot starch as a substitute for cornstarch to thicken sauces. I also use it in combination with other flours to lighten the texture of baked goods. My preferred brand is *Bob's Red Mill*.

- *AVOCADO OIL:* I use avocado oil whenever I can't use olive oil. For instance, when baking at high temperatures (over 350° F) or when the more pungent taste of olive oil would be too strong for the preparation (as with AIP mayonnaise, page 238). My preferred brand is *Chosen Foods*, which is non-GMO and can be safely heated up to 500° F.

* *BAKING POWDER:* Baking powder is used as a leavening agent in baked goods. Unfortunately, most commercial baking powders contain aluminum and/or cornstarch. The best way to avoid these unwanted additives is to *make your own baking powder by mixing one teaspoon cream of tartar with one half teaspoon baking soda.* Store your homemade baking powder in an airtight container and keep it away from moisture.

* *BALSAMIC VINEGAR:* Made from white grape juice, balsamic vinegar has a rich and complex sweet flavor that can be used to enhance the seasoning of salad dressings, marinades, sauces, and even meat and seafood. I use *Newman's Own Organics*, which can be found in most major grocery stores.

* *CAPERS:* Capers are actually unripened flower buds from a perennial plant native to the Mediterranean. Usually brined in salt or vinegar, they give a lemony burst of flavor to foods. I use capers preserved in sea salt, especially when making French tapenade. Salt-packed capers should be soaked in water and then rinsed a few times to remove excess salt before use.

* *CAROB POWDER (ROASTED):* Carob is commonly used as a chocolate substitute and doesn't contain any caffeine. Be careful to check labels as commercial carob chips and powders often contain barley and/or dairy ingredients. My preferred brand for carob powder is *Chatfield's* and I use it frequently in my desserts. Sadly, I have yet to find an AIP compliant brand of carob chips. If you manage to find one, please let me know!

* *CASSAVA FLOUR:* Made from an entire peeled cassava (also know as yuca or manioc) root, and not to be confused with tapioca, which is made from the extracted, bleached starch of the yuca root, cassava flour is a grain-free, nut-free replacement for wheat flour. It brings a wonderful consistency to baked goods. My preferred brand is *Otto's Naturals*.

* *COCONUT AMINOS:* Coconut aminos are a seasoning sauce very similar to soy sauce. Made from coconut, it can be used anywhere you would use soy

sauce. My preferred brand is *Coconut Secret*, which is 100% organic, soy-free, gluten-free, and non-GMO.

✦ *COCONUT BUTTER (RAW):* Made from puréed coconut flesh, coconut butter is an excellent replacement for traditional nut butters. For the ultimate sweet indulgence, try stuffing a date with coconut butter and savor! I also use it occasionally in desserts. I prefer *Artisana Organics*, which is organic and non-GMO.

✦ *COCONUT FLAKES (UNSWEETENED):* Coconut flakes are made from dehydrated coconut flesh. Always purchase the unsweetened variety as commercial versions contain a lot of added sugar. I love to eat them straight out of the bag as a crunchy snack, but they are also wonderful in desserts and other recipes. I buy them in bulk at my local health food store.

✦ *COCONUT FLOUR:* This versatile flour is made from finely ground dried coconut meat. Its rich texture and natural sweetness is great for baking, but use it sparingly because coconut flour tends to absorb a lot of liquid due to its high fiber content. My preferred brand is *Nutiva*, which is organic and non-GMO.

✦ *COCONUT MILK:* When buying coconut milk, make sure it doesn't contain additives like guar gum or xantham gum, which can alter gut microbiome and should be avoided while on the autoimmune protocol. I use coconut milk to create creamy sauces and soups, as a dairy replacement when baking, and in smoothies. My preferred brands are *Aroy-D*, *Savoy*, and *Natural Value*.

✦ *COCONUT OIL:* Coconut oil is a highly versatile pantry staple. It has a wonderful creamy consistency and is suitable for high temperature cooking and baking. I also use it in my personal care for oil pulling. There are several good brands out there, so when making your selection, look for unrefined, cold-pressed virgin coconut oils. Note that coconut oil will stay solid at normal room temperature. My preferred brand is *Nutiva*, which is organic and non-GMO.

❧ *COCONUT WRAPS:* Coconut wraps are an excellent replacement for tortillas and great to have on hand for an emergency "sandwich." My preferred brand is *Paleo Wraps*.

❧ *DATES:* The most common variety, Medjool dates, can be used as a wonderful natural sweetener in baking or as a snack when you want a little something sweet. Limit your consumption though as they pack a lot of sugar! I purchase mine in bulk at my local health food store.

❧ *DRIED HERBS AND SPICES:* Herbs and spices add flavor and depth to any dish! My favorites are cilantro, herbes de Provence, lavender, oregano, parsley, rosemary, sage, and thyme. Wherever possible, I prefer to use fresh herbs and even grow a few varieties in my vegetable garden. *As a general rule, when substituting fresh herbs for dry, use three times as many fresh.* For example, you can swap one teaspoon dried sage with one tablespoon chopped fresh sage.

❧ *EXTRA-VIRGIN OLIVE OIL:* By far my favorite oil to use in the kitchen, extra-virgin olive oil is suitable for cooking and baking up to 350° F. Always choose extra-virgin, first cold pressed olive oil, sold in a dark glass bottle. Store your olive oil in a cold place away from direct sunlight. I like to rotate the brands of olive oil I use because their taste can vary greatly.

❧ *FISH SAUCE:* Made from fresh black anchovies and salt, fish sauce will give your Asian dishes (or any seafood based recipe) a distinctive umami flavor! My preferred brand is *Red Boat*, which is a pure, first pressed, extra virgin fish sauce.

❧ *GELATIN (UNFLAVORED):* Unflavored powdered gelatin is a wonderful pantry staple. In addition to its many health benefits (joint care, gut health, hair and nail strength), it can also be used in many recipes. I often use gelatin when preparing treats and desserts. It can be used as a replacement for eggs in cookies and cakes and is the secret ingredient for making gummies and fruit terrines! I would, however, recommend using only porcine gelatin when baking, as bovine gelatin has a stronger taste. I use *Great Lakes* (the red can) because the animals they use are grass-fed, which is important to me.

* *HONEY:* Honey is a natural sweetener suitable for those following the autoimmune protocol, but use it sparingly as it is pure sugar. Suitable for baking, sweetening hot and cold drinks, as well as balancing more acidic flavors. Choose raw, local, and organic honey whenever possible.

* *MAPLE SYRUP:* Maple syrup is a natural sweetener with a unique flavor that makes it ideal for baking. Grade B maple syrup is preferable to Grade A as it has a richer, deeper flavor as well as a higher nutrient content. My preferred brand is *Now Real Food*, as it is organic and non-GMO.

* *OLIVES:* I like to keep olives on hand to eat as a savory snack or to use as an ingredient in many dishes. I prefer Kalamata olives for their rich and fruity flavor, especially when preparing French tapenade. They come packed in olive oil and vinegar. Be sure to check the label for sneaky non-AIP ingredients! I like *Mediterranean Organic* brand olives, which are organic and non-GMO.

* *PALM SHORTENING:* I use palm shortening in lieu of butter in baked goods. It is solid at room temperature, odorless, and flavorless. I like the *Spectrum* brand, which is an organic, certified sustainable palm oil. If you can't source palm shortening, try this: *combine six parts coconut cream with one part coconut oil and refrigerate.* Use wherever palm shortening is called for.

* *SEA SALT:* Because I use sea salt so often to bring out the natural flavors of my food, I make sure to buy only the finest. My favorites are *Celtic Sea Salt*, *Himalayan Pink Sea Salt*, and last, but not least, *French Fleur de Sel*. Sea salt is naturally packed with beneficial trace minerals. Whichever sort you choose, make sure it is unbleached, unrefined, and devoid of anti-caking agents and additives.

* *TIGERNUTS:* Tigernuts are not actually nuts, but small root vegetables with a slight nutty flavor. They are delicious as a snack, despite the fact

that they are really hard to chew! I purchase *Organic Gemini* tigernuts, which are organic and non-GMO.

❧ *TIGERNUT FLOUR:* Tigernut flour is a fine powder made of ground tigernuts. Its light taste and similar consistency to wheat flour make it a wonderful flour replacement. As with whole tigernuts, I prefer *Organic Gemini,* which is organic and non-GMO.

❧ *VANILLA:* I use vanilla extract frequently when baking. My preferred brand is *Simply Organic.* The alcohol present in vanilla extract cooks off at high temperatures, but for those who are concerned about this, or for cold preparations, vanilla powder is a good option. It is pricier than vanilla extract, but as you will only use a small amount with each use, it should last quite a while. Make sure there are no added sugar or fillers. When cooking, you may *substitute one half teaspoon vanilla powder for one teaspoon vanilla extract.*

# Cooking Times and Temperatures

| LAMB, OVEN ROASTED AT 325°F | | | | |
|---|---|---|---|---|
| | WEIGHT | APPROXIMATE COOKING TIME (MINUTES PER POUND) | | |
| | | Medium-rare (145°F) | Medium (160°F) | Well done (170°F) |
| WHOLE LEG | 5–7 lbs | 15–20 min | 20–25 min | 25–30 min |
| | 7–9 lbs | 20–25 min | 25–30 min | 30–35 min |
| LEG ROAST (BONELESS) | 4–7 lbs | 20 min | 25 min | 30 min |

| CHICKEN, OVEN BAKED OR ROASTED AT 350°F | | |
|---|---|---|
| | WEIGHT | APPROXIMATE COOKING TIME (TOTAL) |
| WHOLE CHICKEN | 2 ½–3 lbs | 1 ¼–1 ½ hours |
| | 3–4 lbs | 1 ½–1 ¾ hours |
| | 4–6 lbs | 1 ¾–2 hours |

→ *Cook until internal temperature in breast reaches 170°F*

| PORK, OVEN BAKED OR ROASTED AT 350°F | | |
|---|---|---|
| | WEIGHT | APPROXIMATE COOKING TIME (MINUTES PER POUND) |
| PICNIC SHOULDER | 2 ½–3 lbs | 25 min |
| | 3–4 lbs | 25–30 min |

→ *Cook until internal temperature reaches 145°F*

| FISH, BAKED AT 350°F | | |
|---|---|---|
| | WEIGHT OR THICKNESS | APPROXIMATE COOKING TIME (TOTAL) |
| WHOLE FISH | 3–5 lbs | 25–30 min |
| FILLETS | 1–2 in | 10–20 min |

| FISH, PAN-FRIED ON MEDIUM HEAT | | |
|---|---|---|
| | THICKNESS | APPROXIMATE COOKING TIME (TOTAL) |
| FILLETS | ¾ in | 7–9 min |
| | 1 in | 9–10 min |

# Oven Temperature

| GAS | FAHRENHEIT (F°) | CELSIUS (C°) |
|---|---|---|
| ½ | 250 | 120 |
| 1 | 275 | 140 |
| 2 | 300 | 150 |
| 3 | 325 | 170 |
| 4 | 350 | 180 |
| 5 | 375 | 190 |
| 6 | 400 | 200 |
| 7 | 425 | 220 |
| 8 | 450 | 230 |
| 9 | 475 | 240 |

# Liquids

| CUP | TBSP | TSP | FLUID OUNCE | MILLILITERS |
|---|---|---|---|---|
| 1 cup | 16 tbsp | 48 tsp | 8 ounces | 240 ml |
| ¾ cup | 12 tbsp | 36 tsp | 6 ounces | 180 ml |
| ⅔ cup | 11 tbsp | 32 tsp | 5 ounces | 148 ml |
| ½ cup | 8 tbsp | 24 tsp | 4 ounces | 120 ml |
| ⅓ cup | 5 tbsp | 16 tsp | 3 ounces | 80 ml |
| ¼ cup | 4 tbsp | 12 tsp | 2 ounces | 60 ml |
| ⅛ cup | 2 tbsp | 6 tsp | 1 ounces | 30 ml |
| ⅟₁₆ cup | 1 tbsp | 3 tsp | .5 ounce | 15 ml |
| | | 1 tsp | | 5 ml |

*2 cups = 480 ml or 1 pint  ∽  4 cups = 950 ml or 1 quart*

# Length

*½ inch = 13 millimeters  ∽  1 inch = 2.5 centimeters*

# Weights

| IMPERIAL | METRIC |
|---|---|
| ½ ounce | 15 grams |
| ¾ ounce | 20 grams |
| 1 ounce | 28 grams |
| 2 ounces | 60 grams |
| 3 ounces | 85 grams |
| 4 ounces (¼ pound) | 113 grams |
| 5 ounces | 140 grams |
| 6 ounces | 170 grams |
| 7 ounces | 200 grams |
| 8 ounces (½ pound) | 230 grams |
| 9 ounces | 255 grams |
| 10 ounces | 285 grams |
| 11 ounces | 310 grams |
| 12 ounces (¾ pound) | 340 grams |
| 13 ounces | 370 grams |
| 14 ounces | 400 grams |
| 15 ounces | 425 grams |
| 16 ounces (1 pound) | 450 grams |
| 24 ounces | 680 grams |
| 32 ounces (2 pounds) | 900 grams |
| 48 ounces (3 pounds) | 1.4 kilograms |
| 64 ounces (4 pounds) | 1.8 kilograms |

*1 kilogram = 35 ounces or 2.2 pounds  ∽  1 ounce = 28.35 grams  ∽  1 gram = 0.0035 ounces*

# Quick Steaming Tutorial

Cut vegetables into uniform sizes. This will ensure they cook at the same rate. While it is fine to mix different vegetables together, be aware that tender vegetables, like cauliflower, will cook faster than denser root vegetables, like carrots.

For a successful end result, I recommend you take care to not over-steam the vegetables. Check them a few times during the cooking process by inserting the tip of a sharp knife into the thickest part of the vegetable. Remove vegetables from the steamer basket when they are still a little firm as they will continue to cook for a few minutes unless you cool them in ice water.

| EQUIPMENT NEEDED | INSTRUCTIONS |
| --- | --- |
| *cutting board* <br><br> *chef's knife* <br><br> *saucepan with a lid* <br><br> *steamer basket* <br><br> *paring knife* | 1. Cut vegetables into uniform sizes. <br><br> 2. Add 1 inch of water to the pan and insert the steamer basket, ensuring the water level stays under the basket. Cover. <br><br> 3. Bring water to a boil over high heat. <br><br> 4. Add vegetables, cover, and reduce heat to medium. <br><br> 5. Check vegetables regularly and remove from steamer when they still have a little firmness to them. <br><br> 6. Drain water and serve vegetables immediately with a drizzle of olive oil and your favorite seasoning or as indicated in the recipe you are following. |

# No. 1
# APPETIZERS

*Rillettes (Coarse Pork Pâté)* / 62

*Easy Artichokes with Shallot Vinaigrette* / 64

*Creamy Liver Pâté* / 66

*Summer Squash Ribbons* / 68

*Bacon Wrapped Asparagus with
Mint and Basil Pesto* / 70

*Marinated Olives* / 72

*Melon and Prosciutto* / 74

*Garlic and Herb Stuffed Mushrooms* / 76

*Pickled Vegetables* / 78

*Sweet Potato, Bacon, and
Avocado Canapés* / 80

# Rillettes (Coarse Pork Pâté)

*Serve this rustic pâté on Crisp Oregano Crackers (page 231) or thin slices of cucumber for a tasty appetizer or an afternoon snack. It partners well with tangy cornichons, grapes, and carrots, but the possibilities are really only limited by your imagination!*

Prep time: 10 minutes + refrigeration ❧ Cook time: 3½ hours ❧ Yield: 1½ cups

## INGREDIENTS

1 pound pork belly, skinned, cut into
1-inch cubes

3 sprigs fresh thyme

1 sprig fresh rosemary

1 bay leaf

1 clove garlic, minced

½ teaspoon fine sea salt

2 cups water

## INSTRUCTIONS

1. In a large skillet, combine all ingredients and bring to a boil. Lower heat to medium–low and continue to simmer, covered, until meat separates easily with a fork, about 3½ hours. It is important that water does not fully evaporate; you may have to add water to ensure meat stays moist.

2. Remove from heat and allow to cool. Once cool, discard herbs and strain meat, reserving liquids.

3. Shred meat using two forks. Check seasoning and adjust salt to taste. (Keep in mind that food served cold needs more salt.)

4. Pack meat into a glass jar, leaving some space at the top. Pour reserved cooking liquid over meat to cover. Discard any unused liquid. Seal the container and chill in the refrigerator for 12 hours.

NOTE: *Will keep in the refrigerator up to 7 days.*

# Easy Artichokes with Shallot Vinaigrette

*Growing up, artichokes were one of my favorite foods. To this day, I love dipping the petals into a zingy vinaigrette and slowly savoring my way to the heart—the best part of the artichoke in my opinion!*

Prep time: 5 minutes  ❧  Cook time: 45 minutes  ❧  Yield: 4 servings

## INGREDIENTS

4 large artichokes

Shallot Vinaigrette (page 242)

## INSTRUCTIONS

1. Trim hard stems to the base of each artichoke.

2. Fill a large saucepan with water and bring to a boil over medium heat. Carefully place artichokes into boiling water and cook until artichoke petals are easily removed, about 45 minutes.

3. Serve warm or cold with shallot vinaigrette on the side.

NOTE: *Peel away the petals and dip them into the shallot vinaigrette. When you reach the center, remove the choke (white thread-like part) and dip the heart into the vinaigrette as well! It's so good!*

# Creamy Liver Pâté

*I first tasted liver as a small child on my grandmother's farm and I have enjoyed eating it ever since. It is also a nutritional powerhouse and because of this, plays an important part in the Paleo Autoimmune Protocol. This version is very user-friendly (creamy, with a soft liver taste) and will be perfect if you are a first-time tester!*

Prep time: 20 minutes + refrigeration  ❧  Cook time: 20 minutes  ❧  Yield: 2⅓ cups

## INGREDIENTS

1 pound chicken or beef liver

⅓ cup bacon fat

1 medium green apple, peeled, cored, and finely chopped

¾ cup white sweet potato, peeled and finely chopped

½ cup finely chopped shallots

2 tablespoons apple cider vinegar

2½ teaspoons dried thyme

2 teaspoons dried rosemary

1 teaspoon fine sea salt

NOTE: *Lard may be substituted for bacon fat. Will keep in the refrigerator up to 3 days. This pâté also freezes well.*

## INSTRUCTIONS

1. Wash liver and pat dry. With a paring knife, trim any white sinew and chop liver into ½-inch pieces.

2. In a large skillet, melt bacon fat over medium heat.

3. Add apple, sweet potato, shallots, and vinegar. Cover and cook, stirring occasionally, until vegetables soften, about 10 to 12 minutes.

4. Add liver, thyme, rosemary, and sea salt. Continue to cook, uncovered and stirring frequently, until liver is cooked through, but still slightly pink inside, about 6 to 8 minutes.

5. Remove from heat and allow to cool.

6. Transfer ingredients to a blender or food processor, making sure to include all cooking juices, and mix until smooth and creamy. You may have to do this in two batches.

7. Check seasoning and adjust salt to taste. (Keep in mind that food served cold needs more salt.)

8. Transfer pâté into small containers and refrigerate until needed.

# Summer Squash Ribbons

*This deliciously healthy and elegant appetizer is also a feast for the eyes. It does require a little bit of preparation, but it is totally worth it!*

Prep time: 20 minutes ❧ Cook time: 30 minutes ❧ Yield: 4 servings

## INGREDIENTS

1 medium yellow summer squash (about ½ pound)

1 medium zucchini (about ½ pound)

½ cup full fat coconut milk

1 tablespoon extra-virgin olive oil

¼ teaspoon dried thyme

Pinch fine sea salt

\* I use a small (6-inch diameter) ceramic dish to bake and serve this appetizer.

## INSTRUCTIONS

1. Heat oven to 350° F. Set the rack in the middle of the oven.

2. Trim tops and bottoms of yellow squash and zucchini. Using a vegetable peeler, cut thin slices from each squash, stopping when you reach the seedy inner core.

3. Roll slices tightly and place in the bottom of the dish, alternating between green and yellow, until the dish is full.

4. Drizzle coconut milk and olive oil over vegetables and sprinkle evenly with thyme and sea salt.

5. Bake until tender, about 30 minutes. Serve hot.

# Bacon Wrapped Asparagus with Mint and Basil Pesto

*Served with a smooth, creamy pesto for dipping, fresh, tender asparagus is the star of the show. Or is it the bacon? In any case, don't be shy and use your hands to savor this tasty appetizer!*

Prep time: 25 minutes ⁊ Cook time: 20 minutes ⁊ Yield: 3-4 servings

## INGREDIENTS

*15 asparagus spears (about 1 pound), ends trimmed*

*15 slices bacon*

*Mint and Basil Pesto (page 224)*

## INSTRUCTIONS

1. Heat oven to 400° F. Set the rack in the middle of the oven.

2. Wrap each asparagus spear in a slice of bacon and lay flat on a baking sheet, ensuring they don't overlap.

3. Bake until bacon is browned to your liking and asparagus spears are tender, about 20 minutes.

4. Enjoy bacon wrapped asparagus warm, dipped in pesto!

# Marinated Olives

*Served as an appetizer or mid-afternoon snack, marinated olives are always a pleasure to eat. As a child, I didn't care much for their bitter taste, but I have since grown to love them. Along with fresh garlic, they represent quintessential French Provençal cuisine for me.*

---

Prep time: 10 minutes + 8 hours marinating ❧ Cook time: n/a ❧ Yield: 2 cups

---

## INGREDIENTS

1 cup pitted green olives

1 cup pitted Kalamata olives

1 tablespoon finely chopped fresh basil

2½ teaspoons finely chopped fresh rosemary

2 cloves garlic, minced

4 tablespoons extra-virgin olive oil

½ tablespoon apple cider vinegar

## INSTRUCTIONS

1. Combine all ingredients in a glass or ceramic dish and marinate in the refrigerator for at least eight hours, stirring occasionally.

2. Remove olives from the refrigerator one hour before serving to allow them to come to room temperature.

---

NOTE: *Will keep in the refrigerator up to 10 days.*

# Melon and Prosciutto

*A classic appetizer. This delicious combination is very easy to put together, yet elegant enough to serve for holiday meals and celebrations!*

Prep time: 10 minutes  &  Cook time: n/a  &  Yield: 4 servings

## INGREDIENTS

1 ripe cantaloupe

8 slices prosciutto

2 cups arugula

Balsamic vinegar, for drizzling

Chopped fresh basil, for garnish

## INSTRUCTIONS

1. Cut cantaloupe in half lengthwise and carefully scoop out seeds with a spoon.

2. Cut each half into four equal crescents and remove the rind. You will have eight pieces total.

3. Onto each plate, arrange ½ cup arugula, two slices melon, and two slices prosciutto.

4. To serve, drizzle plates with vinegar and garnish with fresh basil.

# Garlic and Herb Stuffed Mushrooms

*Stuffed mushrooms are a popular appetizer. Tasty and healthy, they also smell wonderful while baking!*

Prep time: 10 minutes ❧ Cook time: 30 minutes ❧ Yield: 10 mushrooms

## INGREDIENTS

*3 tablespoons extra-virgin olive oil, divided + extra for greasing the dish*

*10 medium white mushrooms (about ¾ pound)*

*4 large cloves garlic, minced*

*1 teaspoon Herbes de Provence (page 232)*

*Pinch fine sea salt*

*\* Special equipment needed: blender or food processor*

## INSTRUCTIONS

1. Heat oven to 350° F. Set the rack in the top level of the oven. Grease the bottom of a baking dish with olive oil.

2. With a paring knife, carefully remove mushroom stems. Combine stems in a blender or food processor with garlic, herbes de Provence, two tablespoons olive oil, and a pinch of sea salt. Mix until you obtain a smooth paste.

3. Stuff mushroom caps with blended paste and arrange in a single layer on the baking dish. Drizzle with remaining tablespoon olive oil and sprinkle with a second pinch of sea salt.

4. Bake until mushrooms are tender, about 30 minutes.

NOTE: *If you have extra stuffing, it tastes great on grilled lamb or beef!*

# Pickled Vegetables

*These pickled vegetables are so pretty and healthy. They make a wonderful and economical homemade gift for any occasion. I prefer to use a wide mouth jar for this recipe because it provides easier access to the vegetables. Enjoy these as an appetizer, over salad, or with grilled meat.*

Prep time: 15 minutes + refrigeration ❧ Cook time: 5 minutes ❧ Yield: 1 (24-ounce) jar

## INGREDIENTS

¾ cup thinly sliced carrots

¾ cup thinly sliced cauliflower florets

¾ cup thinly sliced cucumber

¾ cup thinly sliced radishes

2 cloves garlic, thinly sliced

1 (1-inch) knob fresh ginger, peeled and thinly sliced

For the pickling liquid:

1 cup water

1 cup apple cider vinegar

½ teaspoon fine sea salt

\* *I use a 24-ounce glass jar for this recipe. If your jar is a different size, simply adjust the amount of vegetables and liquid needed to fill the vessel to the brim. The pickling liquid is a mix of 50% water and 50% apple cider vinegar, with ½ teaspoon sea salt for every 2 cups of liquid.*

## INSTRUCTIONS

1. Add all vegetables, including garlic and ginger, to a large bowl. Mix well. Once vegetables are mixed, pack tightly into a 24-ounce jar, or your chosen vessel.

2. In a small saucepan, bring water, vinegar, and sea salt to a rolling boil. Remove from heat and allow to cool.

3. Carefully pour pickling liquid over vegetables, filling the jar all the way to the brim.

4. Affix the lid to the jar and, when cool, chill in the refrigerator for at least 24 hours. Keep refrigerated.

NOTE: *Will keep in the refrigerator for up to 8 days.*

# Sweet Potato, Bacon, and Avocado Canapés

*I was inspired by one of my favorite breakfast combinations when creating this recipe. The flavors marry well and are a crowd favorite. When served as a starter to your meal, I advise serving only one or two per person as these canapés are quite rich and filling!*

Prep time: 10 minutes ❧ Cook time: 20 minutes ❧ Yield: 16 pieces

## INGREDIENTS

*1 medium sweet potato (about ⅔ pound)*

*6 slices bacon*

*2 medium avocados, just ripe*

*3 tablespoons lemon juice*

*Fine sea salt*

*Roughly chopped fresh parsley, for garnish*

## INSTRUCTIONS

1. Peel and chop sweet potato into 1-inch pieces (about 16). Steam until sweet potato is tender, about 20 minutes.

2. In a large skillet, fry bacon over medium heat until cooked, but not crispy, about 10 minutes. Slice into 1-inch squares.

3. Slice avocados in half, remove pits. Carefully spoon out flesh of each half in one piece and chop into 1-inch pieces.

4. In a small bowl, combine avocado pieces and lemon juice. Mix well, making sure to coat all pieces of avocado with lemon juice. (This prevents avocado from oxidizing and turning brown.)

5. To serve, arrange sweet potato cubes on a small tray and sprinkle with sea salt.

6. Top each sweet potato with two pieces bacon, followed by one piece avocado. Finish with parsley for garnish and include a stack of small skewers near the plate.

NOTE: *For my tutorial on steaming, refer to page 58.*

# Niçoise Salad

*This salad of tuna and assorted vegetables is extremely popular in France. You can order it in every little bistro you find across the country. To make this salad AIP compliant, I have replaced the traditional green beans with asparagus. Niçoise salad looks great served on a large platter where guests can help themselves.*

Prep time: 15 minutes  ❧  Cook time: 15 minutes  ❧  Yield: 4 servings

## INGREDIENTS

*1 small white sweet potato (about ½ pound), peeled and chopped*

*⅓ pound asparagus, trimmed*

*1 head Bibb lettuce*

*2 cans (5-ounces each) tuna, drained*

*½ small cucumber (about ¼ pound), peeled and sliced*

*6 medium radishes (about ¼ pound), chopped*

*½ cup black olives*

*Basic Vinaigrette (page 242) or*

*Aïoli (page 240)*

## INSTRUCTIONS

1. Steam sweet potatoes until tender, about eight to nine minutes. Allow to cool.

2. Steam asparagus until tender, about five to six minutes.

3. Put salad together on a serving platter or four plates, starting with lettuce at the bottom. Continue by arranging sweet potatoes, asparagus, tuna, cucumber, radishes, and olives in an attractive fashion.

4. Drizzle with dressing of choice right before serving.

NOTE: *For my tutorial on steaming, refer to page 58.*

# Dandelion Leaf Salad

*For the longest time, I was wary of dandelion leaves. Sounds like rabbit food, right? As it turns out, they make the most delicious salad!*

Prep time: 5 minutes  ◦  Cook time: 10 minutes  ◦  Yield: 4 servings

## INGREDIENTS

*4 slices bacon, chopped*

*½ pound dandelion leaves*

*2 medium, ripe avocados, peeled and chopped*

*Basic Vinaigrette (page 242) or*

*Basic Mayonnaise (page 238)*

## INSTRUCTIONS

1. In a skillet over medium heat, cook bacon until crispy, about 10 minutes.

2. Trim lower part of dandelion stems (about 3–4 inches).

3. Arrange dandelion leaves on a serving platter, top with avocado and crispy bacon.

4. Toss with dressing of choice right before serving.

SERVE WITH: *Sage Roast Chicken (page 150), Herbed Roast Lamb (page 152), Rustic Beef and Pork Meatloaf (page 160), Pork Shoulder Picnic Roast (page 162), Grilled Lamb Chops (page 165), Meatballs with Nomato Sauce (page 168), Baked Cod with Black Olive Tapenade (page 174), Grilled Shrimp with Aïoli (page 178), or Oven-Baked Snapper with Fennel (page 184).*

# Colorful and Fruity Fennel Salad

*Refreshing and uplifting, this fennel salad pairs well with grilled or roasted fish. This is a big salad, well suited for potlucks, picnics, and buffets.*

Prep time: 30 minutes  &  Cook time: n/a  &  Yield: 8 servings

## INGREDIENTS

½ cantaloupe, peeled, deseeded, and cut into 1-inch pieces

3 kiwi fruit, peeled and thinly sliced

1 medium golden beet (about ⅓ pound), cooked, peeled, and thinly sliced

1 medium fennel bulb (about ¼ pound), thinly sliced

1 medium yellow summer squash (about ½ pound), roughly chopped

5 scallions, roughly chopped

3 tablespoons chopped fresh cilantro

Shallot Vinaigrette (page 242) <u>or</u>

Strawberry Vinaigrette (page 242)

## INSTRUCTIONS

1. Combine all ingredients, except dressing, in a large bowl. Mix well.

2. Toss with dressing of choice right before serving.

SERVE WITH: *Sage Roast Chicken (page 150), Pork Shoulder Picnic Roast (page 162), Grilled Shrimp with Aïoli (page 178), Pan-Seared Salmon with Sweet and Sour Vegetables (page 182), or Oven-Baked Snapper with Fennel (page 184).*

# Crunchy Red Cabbage and Kale Salad

*The bright tartness of the apples brings a welcome contrast to the strong "green" taste of the cabbage and kale. This dish will bring a nice touch of color to any meal.*

Prep time: 10 minutes ❧ Cook time: n/a ❧ Yield: 4 servings

## INGREDIENTS

*½ medium red cabbage (about ¾ pound), thinly sliced*

*2 cups tightly packed chopped kale*

*1 medium Granny Smith apple, quartered, cored, and thinly sliced*

*3 scallions, chopped*

*Basic Vinaigrette (page 242) or*

*Basic Mayonnaise (page 238)*

## INSTRUCTIONS

1. Combine all ingredients, except dressing, in a large bowl. Mix well.

2. Toss with dressing of choice right before serving.

SERVE WITH: *Sage Roast Chicken (page 150), Herbed Roast Lamb (page 152), Rustic Beef and Pork Meatloaf (page 160), Pork Shoulder Picnic Roast (page 162), Grilled Lamb Chops (page 164), Lavender and Honey Pork Medallions (page 166), Baked Cod with Black Olive Tapenade (page 174), or Oven-Baked Snapper with Fennel (page 184).*

# Shrimp and Citrus Salad

*Seafood lovers will feast on this shrimp-tastic salad! Pre-cooked shrimp make it a snap, but remember, if you are using frozen shrimp, thaw them beforehand!*

Prep time: 10 minutes  ❧  Cook time: n/a  ❧  Yield: 4 servings

## INGREDIENTS

8 cups chopped romaine lettuce

2 cups chopped radicchio

1 large red grapefruit, peeled and cut into bite-sized pieces

2 cups (about ½ pound) cooked salad shrimp

12 cooked jumbo shrimp (about ½ pound), peeled

2 scallions, chopped

Basic Mayonnaise (page 238) <u>or</u>

Aïoli (page 240)

## INSTRUCTIONS

1. Arrange ingredients on a serving platter in the following order: romaine lettuce, radicchio, grapefruit, salad shrimp, jumbo shrimp, and scallions.

2. Drizzle with dressing of choice right before serving.

# Endive, Pear, and Spinach Salad

*This salad combination was a staple at my house when I was growing up in Belgium. Endive is so popular in that little corner of Europe, that it is often known as "Belgian endive." It pairs deliciously with spinach and pears.*

Prep time: 10 minutes ❦ Cook time: n/a ❦ Yield: 4–5 servings

## INGREDIENTS

4 cups fresh baby spinach

4 cups Belgian endives (3 medium endives), chopped

2 medium pears, peeled, cored, and thinly sliced

1 scallion, chopped

Basic Vinaigrette (page 242) <u>or</u>

Basic Mayonnaise (page 238)

## INSTRUCTIONS

1.  Combine all ingredients, except dressing, in a large bowl. Mix well.

2.  Toss with dressing of choice right before serving.

---

SERVE WITH: *Sage Roast Chicken (page 150), Herbed Roast Lamb (page 152), Rustic Beef and Pork Meatloaf (page 160), Pork Shoulder Picnic Roast (page 162), Grilled Lamb Chops (page 164), Lavender and Honey Pork Medallions (page 166), Baked Cod with Black Olive Tapenade (page 174), Oven-Baked Snapper with Fennel (page 184), or Seared Scallops with Persillade (page 186).*

# Vibrant Pork Belly Salad

*This gorgeous salad is sure to attract "ooohs and aaahs" around the table! Both colorful and nourishing, this is one of my favorites to serve as a fancy lunch option.*

Prep time: 20 minutes   Cook time: 35 minutes   Yield: 4 servings

## INGREDIENTS

1 pound pork belly, skinned and cut into ½-inch cubes

1 tablespoon Herbes de Provence (page 232)

¾ teaspoon fine sea salt

1 tablespoon extra-virgin olive oil

¼ pound arugula

½ pound strawberries, stemmed and quartered

1 medium peach, sliced

1 medium avocado, peeled and sliced

⅓ cup scallions, chopped

Chopped fresh cilantro, for garnish

Basic Vinaigrette (page 242) <u>or</u>

Strawberry Vinaigrette (page 242)

## INSTRUCTIONS

1. Heat oven to 400° F. Set the rack in the middle of the oven.

2. Combine pork belly, herbes de Provence, sea salt, and olive oil in a bowl. Mix well.

3. Spread pork evenly on a baking sheet and bake until cooked through, about 35 minutes, turning once.

4. Arrange ingredients on a serving platter in the following order: arugula, strawberries, peach slices, avocado, pork belly, and scallions. Garnish with fresh cilantro.

5. Drizzle with dressing of choice right before serving.

# Kale and Ginger Salad

*Kale and ginger—two nutritional powerhouses. This salad gives you extra points for being super healthy!*

Prep time: 15 minutes  ☙  Cook time: n/a  ☙  Yield: 4–5 servings

## INGREDIENTS

½ pound kale, ribs removed and roughly chopped

1 medium avocado, peeled and sliced

¼ cup fresh parsley, roughly chopped

2 scallions, roughly chopped

1 tablespoon grated fresh ginger

Basic Mayonnaise (page 238) <u>or</u>

Avocado Mayonnaise (page 238)

## INSTRUCTIONS

1. Arrange ingredients on a serving platter in the following order: kale, avocado, parsley, scallions, and ginger.

2. Drizzle with dressing of choice right before serving.

SERVE WITH: *Sage Roast Chicken (page 150), Rustic Beef and Pork Meatloaf (page 160), Pork Shoulder Picnic Roast (page 162), Oven-Baked Turmeric Tilapia (page 176), or Oven-Baked Snapper with Fennel (page 184).*

# Leftover Chicken Salad

*I don't know about you, but whenever I roast a whole chicken I always end up with leftovers. The problem is, there are never enough to feed the entire family a whole second meal, so I turn them into a colorful salad instead!*

Prep time: 15 minutes  ~  Cook time: n/a  ~  Yield: 4 servings

## INGREDIENTS

8 cups tightly packed mixed greens of choice

2 medium carrots (about ⅓ pound), thinly sliced

8 medium radishes (about ⅓ pound), thinly sliced

1 medium watermelon radish (2-inch diameter), thinly sliced

½ pound leftover cooked chicken, chopped

3 scallions, chopped

Basic Mayonnaise (page 238) <u>or</u>

Avocado Mayonnaise (page 238)

## INSTRUCTIONS

1. Arrange ingredients on a serving platter in the following order: mixed greens, carrots, radishes, watermelon radish, chicken, and scallions.

2. Drizzle with dressing of choice right before serving.

# Afternoon Snack Salad

*This colorful and refreshing salad can be served as a meal accompaniment or divided into smaller portions for a salad "on-the-go." I like to munch on the big pieces of vegetables for a healthy, low-carb snack. Choose your favorite dressing as a dip!*

Prep time: 10 minutes  ๑  Cook time: n/a  ๑  Yield: 4 servings

## INGREDIENTS

8 cups green lettuce, finely chopped

1 small cucumber (about ⅓ pound), thinly sliced

1 small yellow summer squash (about ⅓ pound), thinly sliced

4 small young carrots (about ⅓ pound), peeled

8 medium radishes (about ⅓ pound), chopped

4 scallions

Roughly chopped fresh parsley, for garnish

Basic Mayonnaise (page 238) <u>or</u>

Avocado Mayonnaise (page 238)

## INSTRUCTIONS

1. Arrange all ingredients on a serving platter or divide between four smaller portions.

2. Include dressing of choice on the side, for dipping.

No. 3
SOUPS

# Watercress and Spinach Soup

*I particularly love the earthy flavor of watercress in this simple soup. The addition of coconut milk makes it rich and creamy.*

Prep time: 10 minutes  ❧  Cook time: 35 minutes  ❧  Yield: 2½ quarts / 5 (16-ounce) servings

## INGREDIENTS

*1 small cauliflower (about 1 pound), chopped*

*2 quarts Chicken Bone Broth (page 234)*

*6 ounces watercress, roughly chopped*

*5 ounces fresh spinach, roughly chopped*

*½ cup full fat coconut milk + extra for garnish*

*Fine sea salt*

*Chopped fresh cilantro, for garnish*

*\* Special equipment needed: immersion blender*

## INSTRUCTIONS

1. Add cauliflower and chicken broth to a large stockpot. Bring to a boil, then lower heat to medium and cook, covered, for 15 minutes.

2. Add watercress and spinach. Continue to cook, covered, until vegetables are tender, about 10 more minutes.

3. Remove from heat and mix thoroughly with an immersion blender until smooth.

4. Stir in coconut milk. Season to taste with salt.

5. Serve hot with a drizzle of coconut milk and a garnish of fresh cilantro.

NOTE: *Will keep in the refrigerator for up to 5 days.*

# French Onion Soup

*Since onions are readily available all year long, there is no reason you can't enjoy this hearty French soup any time. In this version, I replace the traditional bread and cheese garnish with savory fried onions and crispy bacon!*

---

Prep time: 20 minutes ❧ Cook time: 35 minutes ❧ Yield: 3 quarts / 6 (16-ounce) servings

---

## INGREDIENTS

*2½ pounds yellow onions, peeled and chopped + 2 medium yellow onions for garnish, peeled and thinly sliced*

*1 small cauliflower (about 1 pound), chopped*

*2 quarts Chicken Bone Broth (page 234)*

*8 slices bacon, thinly sliced*

*Fine sea salt*

*\* Special equipment needed: immersion blender*

## INSTRUCTIONS

1. Add chopped onion, cauliflower, and chicken broth to a large stockpot. Bring to a boil, then reduce heat to medium and cook, covered, until vegetables are tender, about 20 minutes.

2. While vegetables are cooking, place bacon in a large skillet. Cover and cook over medium heat, stirring frequently, until brown and crispy, about 8 to 10 minutes.

3. Using a slotted spoon, transfer bacon to a paper towel-lined plate to drain. Reserve bacon fat. Add thinly sliced onion to the skillet and cook, covered, on medium heat for about 15 to 20 minutes, stirring frequently. Onions should be brown and crispy, but not burnt!

4. When vegetables for the soup are tender, remove from heat and mix thoroughly with an immersion blender until smooth.

5. Season to taste with salt. Serve soup hot with fried onions and bacon for garnish.

---

NOTE: *Will keep in the refrigerator for up to 5 days.*

# Butternut Squash and Sweet Potato Soup

*This golden-hued soup is a favorite at my house. The addition of sweet potatoes makes it extra nourishing. For an even heartier meal, add a little sautéed ground beef to each serving.*

Prep time: 15 minutes ❧ Cook time: 35 minutes ❧ Yield: 3 quarts / 6 (16-ounce) servings

## INGREDIENTS

2 pounds chopped butternut squash

1 large sweet potato (about ¾ pound), peeled and chopped

1 medium red onion (about ½ pound), peeled and chopped

2 quarts Chicken Bone Broth (page 234)

Fine sea salt

Chopped fresh basil, for garnish

\* Special equipment needed: immersion blender

## INSTRUCTIONS

1. Add squash, sweet potatoes, red onion, and broth to a large stockpot. Bring to a boil, then reduce heat to medium and cook, covered, until vegetables are tender, about 20 to 25 minutes.

2. Remove from heat and mix thoroughly with an immersion blender until smooth.

3. Season to taste with salt. Serve hot with a garnish of fresh basil.

NOTE: *Will keep in the refrigerator for up to 5 days.*

# Hearty Green Cabbage Soup

*Cabbage may not be on your list of "sexiest vegetables," but I promise you, this hearty soup is far greater than the sum of its parts. And it tastes even better the next day! This is one of my absolute favorite soups to eat for a tummy-warming breakfast.*

Prep time: 15 minutes  ℘  Cook time: 50 minutes  ℘  Yield: 3½ quarts / 7 (16-ounce) servings

## INGREDIENTS

1 small green cabbage (about 2½ pounds)

3 tablespoons extra-virgin olive oil

¾ pound bacon, cut into ½-inch strips

1 large turnip (about 1 pound), diced

1 large leek (about ¾ pound), washed and thinly sliced

1 medium yellow onion (about ½ pound), peeled and thinly sliced

2 cloves of garlic, minced

2 quarts Chicken Bone Broth (page 234)

1 bay leaf

Fine sea salt

Chopped fresh parsley, for garnish

## INSTRUCTIONS

1.  Cut cabbage in half. Remove and discard outer leaves and core. Chop cabbage into ¼-inch slices.

2.  Heat olive oil in a large stockpot. Add cabbage, bacon, turnip, leek, onion, and garlic. Cover and cook on medium-high heat, stirring occasionally, until vegetables are wilted, about 10 minutes.

3.  Add chicken broth and bay leaf. Bring to a boil, then reduce heat to medium and cook, covered, until vegetables are tender, about 25 to 30 minutes.

4.  Discard bay leaf. Season to taste with salt. Garnish with fresh parsley.

NOTE: *Will keep in the refrigerator for up to 5 days.*

# Vichyssoise

*Vichyssoise is a world-renowned French soup usually served chilled or at room temperature. Light and easy to prepare, this is the perfect soup for a summer lunch! The recipe calls for only the white part of leeks. I keep the green parts to whip up a quick breakfast casserole the next morning.*

Prep time: 15 minutes ❧ Cook time: 25 minutes ❧ Yield: 3½ quarts / 7 (16-ounce) servings

## INGREDIENTS

4 tablespoons extra-virgin olive oil

1 pound leeks, white part only (from 4 large leeks), washed and thinly sliced

3 English cucumbers (about 2 pounds), peeled, seeded, and chopped

¾ pound cauliflower florets, chopped (1 small cauliflower)

2 quarts Chicken Bone Broth (page 234)

1½ teaspoons fine sea salt

½ cup full fat coconut milk + extra for garnish

Chopped fresh chives, for garnish

\* Special equipment needed: immersion blender

---

NOTE: *To seed a cucumber, slice the cucumber in half lengthwise. Run a spoon down the middle, scooping out the seeds as you go. Will keep in the refrigerator for up to 5 days.*

---

## INSTRUCTIONS

1. In a large stockpot, heat olive oil over medium–high heat. Add leeks and sauté, uncovered, for five minutes, stirring frequently. Take care that leeks don't stick to the bottom of the pot or turn brown.

2. Add cucumber, cauliflower, chicken broth, and sea salt. Cover and bring to a boil. Lower heat to medium and cook, covered, until vegetables are tender, about 10 minutes.

3. Remove from heat and mix thoroughly with an immersion blender until smooth.

4. Add coconut milk. Check the seasoning and adjust salt to taste. (Keep in mind that food served cold needs more salt.)

5. Refrigerate about four hours or until thoroughly chilled.

6. Serve with a swirl of coconut milk and a garnish of fresh chives.

# Country-Style Chicken Soup

*The addition of bacon gives this traditional chicken and vegetable soup a welcome smoky flavor. You can prepare this hearty soup ahead of time; it will taste even better after the flavors have time to combine!*

Prep time: 30 minutes  ❧  Cook time: 30 minutes  ❧  Yield: 3½ quarts / 7 (16-ounce) servings

## INGREDIENTS

1 pound carrots, peeled and finely chopped

½ pound celery, finely chopped

½ pound leeks, washed and finely chopped

½ pound turnip, diced

2 cloves garlic, minced

2 whole cloves

1 bay leaf

2½ quarts Chicken Bone Broth (page 234)

½ pound bacon, thinly sliced

1 pound chicken breasts, cut into bite-sized pieces

Fine sea salt

## INSTRUCTIONS

1. Add carrots, celery, leeks, turnip, garlic, cloves, bay leaf, and chicken broth to a large stockpot. Bring to a boil, then reduce heat to medium and cook, covered, until vegetables are tender, about 15 to 20 minutes.

2. Meanwhile, in a large skillet over medium heat, cook bacon, uncovered, until brown, about 10 minutes. Transfer bacon to a paper towel-lined plate with a slotted spoon and set aside.

3. In the same skillet, add chicken and cook in bacon fat, covered, until tender, about 7 to 10 minutes.

4. Add chicken and bacon to soup. Season to taste with salt and serve hot.

NOTE: *Will keep in the refrigerator for up to 5 days.*

# Asparagus and Zucchini Soup

*Zucchini is available all year long and grows abundantly in gardens during the summer. It has a mild, neutral taste that marries well with other vegetables. In this case, the velvety zucchini is enhanced by the distinctive quality of fresh asparagus.*

Prep time: 15 minutes ❧ Cook time: 30 minutes ❧ Yield: 3½ quarts / 7 (16-ounce) servings

## INGREDIENTS

*2 pounds green asparagus*

*2 pounds zucchini, chopped*

*2 quarts Chicken Bone Broth (page 234)*

*Fine sea salt*

*Chopped fresh mint, for garnish*

*Extra-virgin olive oil, for garnish*

*\* Special equipment needed: immersion blender*

## INSTRUCTIONS

1. Trim ends of asparagus with a kitchen knife and discard. Cut off tips of asparagus and reserve. Roughly chop remaining stems.

2. Add asparagus stems, zucchini, and chicken broth to a stockpot. Bring to a boil, then reduce heat to medium-low and cook, covered, until vegetables are tender, about 20 minutes.

3. Meanwhile, steam asparagus tips until tender, but not mushy, about five minutes. Transfer to a bowl and set aside.

4. Remove soup from heat and mix thoroughly with an immersion blender until smooth.

5. Season to taste with salt. Serve with a garnish of asparagus tips, fresh mint, and a drizzle olive oil.

NOTE: *For my tutorial on steaming, refer to page 58. Will keep in the refrigerator for up to 5 days.*

# Slow Cooker Chicken Soup with Avocado and Scallions

*This easy, nutrient-dense soup is one of my staples. I place the chicken in the slow cooker at night, right before going to bed, and enjoy this soup for breakfast. Save the carcass and bones from the bird to make more bone broth.*

Prep time: 10 minutes ❧ Cook time: 10 hours ❧ Yield: 3 quarts / 6 (16-ounce) servings

## INGREDIENTS

1 whole chicken

2½ quarts Chicken Bone Broth (page 234) or water

Fine sea salt

*FOR EACH SERVING OF SOUP:*

2 tablespoons chopped fresh cilantro or Italian parsley

2 tablespoons chopped scallions

½ medium avocado, chopped

\* Special equipment needed: 6-quart slow cooker

## INSTRUCTIONS

1. Place chicken and chicken broth (or water) into the slow cooker. Cover and simmer until meat falls off bone, about 8 to 10 hours.

2. Remove chicken from the slow cooker and allow to cool. Using two forks, shred meat, reserving carcass and bones for bone broth.

3. Strain cooking liquid through a fine sieve and return to the slow cooker. Add shredded chicken.

4. Season to taste with salt.

5. For each serving of soup, add two tablespoons fresh herbs, two tablespoons scallions, and chopped avocado. Serve hot.

NOTE: *Will keep in the refrigerator for up to 5 days.*

# Carrot Soup with Lemon and Honey

*This simple soup will surprise you with its combination of carrots, honey, and lemon. Absolutely delectable! To make this soup dinner party worthy just add an additional garnish of finely sliced carrot that has been lightly sautéed in a skillet with a little olive oil. Voilà!*

Prep time: 20 minutes ❧ Cook time: 30 minutes ❧ Yield: 3 quarts / 6 (16-ounce) servings

## INGREDIENTS

*2 pounds carrots, peeled and chopped*

*1 pound yellow onions, peeled and chopped*

*1½ quarts Chicken Bone Broth (page 234)*

*2 cups full fat coconut milk*

*2 tablespoons honey*

*2 tablespoons lemon juice*

*Fine sea salt*

*Chopped fresh parsley, for garnish*

*\* Special equipment needed: immersion blender*

## INSTRUCTIONS

1. Add carrots, onion, and chicken broth to a large stockpot. Bring to a boil, then reduce heat to medium and cook, covered, until vegetables are tender, about 20 minutes.

2. Remove from heat and mix thoroughly with an immersion blender until smooth.

3. Stir in coconut milk, honey, and lemon juice. Season to taste with salt.

4. Serve with a generous garnish of fresh parsley.

NOTE: *Will keep in the refrigerator for up to 5 days.*

# Rainbow Chard, Beef, and Cauliflower Soup

*This is the kind of hearty soup that will warm your tummy any time of the day! If, like me, you don't like to waste any food, you will be right at home using the stems of the chard. They taste wonderful and just need to cook a little bit longer than the soft leaves.*

Prep time: 15 minutes  ❧  Cook time: 30 minutes  ❧  Yield: 4 quarts / 8 (16-ounce) servings

## INGREDIENTS

1 pound rainbow chard

5 tablespoons extra-virgin olive oil, divided

1 large yellow onion (about 1 pound), peeled and chopped

3 large cloves garlic, minced

1 large cauliflower (about 2 pounds), cored and chopped

2 quarts Chicken Bone Broth (page 234)

1 pound ground beef

¾ teaspoon fine sea salt

## INSTRUCTIONS

1. Separate stems from chard leaves. Chop stems into ¼-inch pieces. Roughly chop leaves.

2. In a large stockpot, heat four tablespoons olive oil over medium-high heat. Add chard stems, onion, and garlic. Cook for about 10 minutes, stirring to ensure vegetables don't turn brown or stick to the bottom of the pot.

3. Add cauliflower and chicken broth. Bring to a boil, then reduce heat to medium and continue to cook, covered, until vegetables are tender, about 10 minutes.

4. While vegetables are cooking, heat remaining tablespoon olive oil in a large skillet over medium heat. Add ground beef and sea salt.

5. Cook until meat is brown and cooked through, about 5 minutes. Set aside and keep warm.

6. When vegetables are cooked, turn off heat. Stir in cooked meat and chard leaves. Cover and let sit for 10 minutes.

7. Before serving, check seasoning and adjust salt to taste.

NOTE: *Any type of chard or kale may be substituted for rainbow chard. Will keep in the refrigerator for up to 5 days.*

No. 4

VEGETABLES

# No Nightshade Ratatouille

*As you will undoubtedly want leftovers, it is always a good idea to prepare ratatouille in large quantities. The flavors meld and improve after a couple of days making it even more delicious. Ratatouille can be served chilled as a refreshing summer lunch or hot with grilled or roast lamb, pork, or poultry.*

Prep time: 15 minutes ❧ Cook time: 40 minutes ❧ Yield: 4 servings

## INGREDIENTS

¼ cup extra-virgin olive oil

2 medium golden beets (about ½ pound), peeled and roughly chopped

3 medium carrots (about ½ pound), peeled and roughly chopped

4 cloves garlic, minced

1 large yellow onion (about ¾ pound), peeled and roughly chopped

1 medium yellow summer squash (about ½ pound), chopped

1 medium zucchini (about ½ pound), chopped

1 tablespoon dried oregano

1 tablespoon minced fresh rosemary

1 teaspoon fine sea salt

## INSTRUCTIONS

1. In a large saucepan, heat olive oil over medium-low heat. Add beets, carrots, and garlic. Cover and cook for 20 minutes, stirring occasionally.

2. Add onion, yellow squash, zucchini, oregano, rosemary, and sea salt. Continue cooking, covered, until vegetables are tender, about 20 minutes.

3. Check seasoning and adjust salt to taste. Serve hot or cold.

NOTE: *Add 10–15 minutes to the cooking time if you prefer your ratatouille well-done over crisp-tender.*

SERVE WITH: *Sage Roast Chicken (page 150), Herbed Roast Lamb (page 152), Rustic Beef and Pork Meatloaf (page 160), Pork Shoulder Picnic Roast (page 162), Lavender and Honey Pork Medallions (page 166), Baked Cod with Black Olive Tapenade (page 174), or Oven-Baked Snapper with Fennel (page 184).*

# Oven-Roasted Fennel and Garlic

*The garlic, roasted slowly within its skin, is transformed from pungent vegetable into a deliciously fragrant butter that can be spread on the fennel or anything else nearby! Do not be tempted to peel the garlic before cooking; the outer layers will protect it from burning. Serve this aromatic dish as an accompaniment to any roast or grilled meat.*

Prep time: 10 minutes ❧ Cook time: 60 minutes ❧ Yield: 4 servings

## INGREDIENTS

2 tablespoons extra-virgin olive oil + extra for greasing the dish

4 heads garlic

3 medium fennel bulbs (about ¾ pound)

1 cup Chicken Bone Broth (page 234) + extra if needed

1 sprig rosemary, leaves plucked from the stem

⅛ fine sea salt

## INSTRUCTIONS

1. Heat oven to 350° F. Set the rack in the middle of the oven. Grease the bottom of a baking dish with olive oil.

2. Slice tops off garlic heads to just expose cloves.

3. Trim stems from fennel bulbs and quarter.

4. Arrange fennel and garlic in one layer in the greased dish. Pour chicken broth over vegetables.

5. Drizzle with 2 tablespoons olive oil and season with rosemary leaves and sea salt.

6. Roast until vegetables are tender, basting occasionally, about one hour.

7. Should too much broth evaporate, add a little extra to ensure vegetables don't dry out.

8. Serve warm with your choice of meat or fish.

SERVE WITH: *Sage Roast Chicken (page 150), Herbed Roast Lamb (page 152), Tarragon Provençal Chicken (page 154), Grilled Lamb Chops (page 164), Baked Cod with Black Olive Tapenade (page 174), Oven-Baked Snapper with Fennel (page 184), or Baked Salmon with Lemon and Dill Sauce (page 188).*

# Creamy Broccoli Mash

*This is a magical purée with a rustic feeling. Perfect for using up all those leftover broccoli stems and always a crowd pleaser! For an even creamier mash, simply increase the amount of coconut milk.*

Prep time: 15 minutes ❧ Cook time: 15 minutes ❧ Yield: 3 cups

## INGREDIENTS

1 pound broccoli, chopped

1 small white sweet potato (about ½ pound), peeled and chopped

½ cup full fat coconut milk

Fine sea salt

Finely chopped fresh parsley, for garnish

\* Special equipment needed: blender or food processor

## INSTRUCTIONS

1. Steam broccoli and sweet potatoes until tender, about 15 minutes. Allow to cool for a few minutes.

2. Combine vegetables and coconut milk in a blender or food processor. Mix on low speed until creamy. You may have to do this in two batches.

3. Season to taste with salt.

4. Transfer to a serving dish. Garnish with fresh parsley.

NOTE: *For my tutorial on steaming, refer to page 58.*

SERVE WITH: *Sage Roast Chicken (page 150), Tarragon Provençal Chicken (page 154), Rustic Beef and Pork Meatloaf (page 160), Pork Shoulder Picnic Roast (page 162), Oven-Baked Turmeric Tilapia (page 176), Oven-Baked Snapper with Fennel (page 184), Seared Scallops with Persillade (page 186), or Baked Salmon with Lemon and Dill Sauce (page 188).*

# Roasted Vegetable Medley

*This is a lovely dish to serve on a weeknight. Just pop the vegetables in the oven and serve without any fuss!*

Prep time: 8 minutes ❧ Cook time: 40 minutes ❧ Yield: 4–5 servings

## INGREDIENTS

*2 tablespoons extra-virgin olive oil + extra for greasing the pan*

*1½ pounds cauliflower florets (1 medium cauliflower)*

*2 medium yellow summer squash (about 1 pound), chopped*

*8 large radishes (about ½ pound), chopped*

*1 teaspoon dried thyme*

*½ teaspoon fine sea salt*

## INSTRUCTIONS

1. Heat oven to 350° F. Grease the bottom of a roasting pan with olive oil.

2. Arrange vegetables in the roasting pan and season with 2 tablespoons olive oil, thyme, and sea salt.

3. Bake until vegetables are tender, about 35 to 40 minutes. Stir vegetables once or twice during baking. Serve hot.

SERVE WITH: *Sage Roast Chicken (page 150), Herbed Roast Lamb (page 152), Rustic Beef and Pork Meatloaf (page 160), Pork Shoulder Picnic Roast (page 162), Meatballs with Nomato Sauce (page 168), Baked Cod with Black Olive Tapenade (page 174), Oven-Baked Snapper with Fennel (page 184), or Baked Salmon with Lemon and Dill Sauce (page 188).*

# Balsamic Spaghetti Squash

*To make life a little easier for yourself, consider cooking the spaghetti squash in advance. Then, when you're ready with the topping, simply reheat the squash and serve. Also, this dish is great for leftovers and will keep several days in the refrigerator.*

Prep time: 15 minutes  ❧  Cook time: 45 minutes  ❧  Yield: 5–6 servings

## INGREDIENTS

1 medium spaghetti squash
(about 3 pounds)

½ pound bacon, thinly sliced

1 large red onion (about ¾ pound),
peeled and thinly sliced

1 cup Kalamata olives, pitted and sliced

¼ cup water

½ tablespoon balsamic vinegar

2 teaspoons Herbes de Provence
(page 232)

Extra-virgin olive oil, for garnish

---

SERVE WITH: *Sage Roast Chicken (page 150), Herbed Roast Lamb (page 152), Chicken Livers with Fresh Figs (page 156), Rustic Beef and Pork Meatloaf (page 160), Pork Shoulder Picnic Roast (page 162), Grilled Lamb Chops (page 164), Lavender and Honey Pork Medallions (page 166), or Meatballs with Nomato Sauce (page 168).*

---

## INSTRUCTIONS

1. Heat oven to 400° F. Set the rack in the middle of the oven.

2. Cut off top and bottom of spaghetti squash with a large serrated knife. Slice in half, lengthwise. Scoop out seeds with a spoon. Place two halves face down in a baking dish. Fill the bottom of the dish with one inch of water.

3. Place in the oven and bake until skin softens and gives a little when you push it with your finger, about 30 to 35 minutes.

4. Remove from the oven, drain water, and let cool for a few minutes before handling. With a fork, scrape out flesh of squash, making spaghetti noodles. Set aside and keep warm.

5. In a large skillet, cook bacon over medium heat until brown and crispy, stirring frequently, about 10 to 12 minutes. Transfer bacon to a paper towel-lined plate with a slotted spoon and set aside.

6. Add onion to the skillet and cook in bacon fat until tender and slightly brown, about 8 minutes.

7. Turn heat to low. Add cooked bacon, olives, water, vinegar, and herbes de Provence to the skillet. Cover and cook for five minutes. Check seasoning and adjust salt to taste.

8. Serve spaghetti squash with a generous portion of bacon topping and a drizzle of olive oil.

# Celeriac Remoulade

This remoulade makes perfect use of a very common vegetable in France, the humble celeriac. Less common on this side of the Atlantic, celeriac is both refreshing and earthy in taste. Served with a tasty sauce (of the same name!), this dish will win you over! This dish partners beautifully with fish.

Prep time: 25 minutes + refrigeration  ❧  Cook time: 10 minutes  ❧  Yield: 4 servings

## INGREDIENTS

1 large celeriac (about 2 pounds)

1½ quarts water

⅓ cup lemon juice

⅓ cup minced fresh parsley

¼ cup capers

¼ cup finely chopped gherkins or pickled cucumber

½ teaspoon fine sea salt

Remoulade Sauce (page 241)

---

SERVE WITH: *Pork Shoulder Picnic Roast (page 162), Baked Cod with Black Olive Tapenade (page 174), Grilled Shrimp with Aïoli (page 178), Oven Baked Snapper with Fennel (page 184), or Baked Salmon with Lemon and Dill Sauce (page 188).*

---

## INSTRUCTIONS

1. With a sharp knife, remove and discard tough outer skin of celeriac. Rinse and shred remaining flesh, using a food processor or grater.

2. Place shredded celeriac into a large bowl and immediately cover with water and lemon juice to prevent discoloration. Soak for about 10 minutes.

3. Fill a large saucepan with water and bring to a boil. As it boils, prepare a large bowl of ice water.

4. Drain celeriac, then blanch in boiling water for one minute.

5. Drain celeriac again and immediately plunge into the bowl of ice water to stop the cooking process.

6. Drain again and pat dry using paper towels. Allow to cool completely.

7. In a large bowl, combine cooled shredded celeriac, parsley, capers, gherkins, sea salt, and remoulade sauce. Mix well. Check seasoning and adjust salt to taste.

8. Refrigerate two to four hours or until thoroughly chilled. Serve cold.

# Zingy Beet and Carrot Salad

*Beets and carrots form a lively combination and fresh ginger adds a special flavor to this dish! Red beets can be used for this recipe, but be aware that the entire dish will turn crimson!*

Prep time: 20 minutes + marinade  ❧  Cook time: 35 minutes  ❧  Yield: 4–5 servings

## INGREDIENTS

4 medium Chioggia beets or golden beets (about 1 pound)

5 medium carrots (about 1 pound), peeled and cut into ¼-inch slices

### ❧ MARINADE

Juice of one orange (about ⅓ cup)

1 teaspoon lemon zest

Juice of one lemon (about 4 tablespoons)

1 tablespoon apple cider vinegar

1 tablespoon extra-virgin olive oil

1 teaspoon grated fresh ginger

½ teaspoon fine sea salt

Finely chopped fresh chives, for garnish

## INSTRUCTIONS

1. Place beets in a saucepan and cover with water. Bring to a low boil over medium heat and cook, covered, until beets are tender, about 30 to 35 minutes. Drain and allow to cool.

2. Once cooled, remove skin from beets. Chop into ½-inch pieces.

3. Steam carrots until tender, about 15 to 20 minutes. Drain and allow to cool.

4. In a large glass or ceramic bowl, combine orange juice, lemon zest, lemon juice, vinegar, olive oil, ginger, and sea salt.

5. Add cooked beets and carrots to marinade. Mix well and refrigerate, covered, for at least two hours, stirring occasionally.

6. Immediately before serving, check seasoning and adjust salt to taste. Garnish with fresh chives.

SERVE WITH: *Sage Roast Chicken (page 150), Herbed Roast Lamb (page 152), Chicken Livers with Fresh Figs (page 156), Rustic Beef and Pork Meatloaf (page 160), Pork Shoulder Picnic Roast (page 162), Grilled Lamb Chops (page 164), Lavender and Honey Pork Medallions (page 166), Oven-Baked Turmeric Tilapia (page 176), Grilled Shrimp with Aïoli (page 178), or Seared Scallops with Persillade (page 186).*

# Brussels Sprout Hash

*Brussels sprouts, when properly prepared, are delicious! This rustic casserole is a winner in my household.*

Prep time: 25 minutes ❧ Cook time: 25 minutes ❧ Yield: 4 servings

## INGREDIENTS

3 tablespoons extra-virgin olive oil

1 large sweet potato (about ¾ pound), diced into small cubes

½ pound white mushrooms, sliced

1 small yellow onion (about ⅓ pound), peeled and chopped

½ teaspoon fine sea salt

½ pound Brussels sprouts, shredded

2 scallions, chopped

## INSTRUCTIONS

1. Heat olive oil in a large skillet over medium-high heat. Add sweet potato, mushrooms, onion, and sea salt. Mix well. Cover and cook until vegetables are tender, stirring occasionally, about 25 minutes.

2. Turn off heat and add Brussels sprouts. Mix well.

3. Check seasoning and adjust salt to taste. Serve hot with a garnish of scallions.

SERVE WITH: *Sage Roast Chicken (page 150), Herbed Roast Lamb (page 152), Rustic Beef and Pork Meatloaf (page 160), Pork Shoulder Picnic Roast (page 162), Meatballs with Nomato Sauce (page 168), Oven-Baked Turmeric Tilapia (page 176), or Oven-Baked Snapper with Fennel (page 184).*

# Cauliflower Salad with Scallions

*This dish is the perfect replacement for rice and will pair well with just about any dish. Often seen shredded, or "riced," in Paleo recipes, I prefer to slice the cauliflower florets for a more interesting texture.*

Prep time: 10 minutes  ❧  Cook time: 8 minutes  ❧  Yield: 3–4 servings

## INGREDIENTS

2 pounds cauliflower florets
(1 large cauliflower)

2 tablespoons coconut oil

5 scallions, finely chopped

½ teaspoon fine sea salt

\* Special equipment needed:
  food processor

## INSTRUCTIONS

1. Slice cauliflower florets thinly using the slicing blade attachment of your food processor.

2. Heat coconut oil in a large skillet over medium heat. Add cauliflower, scallions, and sea salt. Mix well. Cover and cook until crisp-tender, about five to eight minutes.

3. Check seasoning and adjust salt to taste. Serve hot.

SERVE WITH: *Sage Roast Chicken (page 150), Herbed Roast Lamb (page 152), Tarragon Provençal Chicken (page 154), Rustic Beef and Pork Meatloaf (page 160), Pork Shoulder Picnic Roast (page 162), Lavender and Honey Pork Medallions (page 166), Meatballs with Nomato Sauce (page 168), Baked Cod with Black Olive Tapenade (page 174), Oven-Baked Turmeric Tilapia (page 176), or Baked Salmon with Lemon and Dill Sauce (page 188).*

# Pan-Fried Sweet Potatoes with Sage

*Prepare this simple and fragrant side dish while your entrée is cooking.*

Prep time: 5 minutes  ❧  Cook time: 20 minutes  ❧  Yield: 4 servings

## INGREDIENTS

2 tablespoons coconut oil

2 large sweet potatoes (about 1½ pounds), peeled and cut into ½-inch pieces

1 tablespoon dried sage

½ teaspoon fine sea salt

## INSTRUCTIONS

1. In a large frying pan, heat coconut oil over medium heat. Add sweet potatoes, sage, and sea salt. Toss to coat.

2. Cover and cook, stirring frequently, until vegetables are tender, about 20 minutes.

3. If sweet potatoes are browning too quickly, add ¼ cup water and reduce heat slightly. Serve hot.

SERVE WITH: *Sage Roast Chicken (page 150), Herbed Roast Lamb (page 152), Chicken Livers with Fresh Figs (page 156), Rustic Beef and Pork Meatloaf (page 160), Pork Shoulder Picnic Roast (page 162), Grilled Lamb Chops (page 164), Lavender and Honey Pork Medallions (page 166), or Pan-Seared Salmon with Sweet and Sour Vegetables (page 182).*

*Sage Roast Chicken* / 150

*Herbed Roast Lamb* / 152

*Tarragon Provençal Chicken* / 154

*Chicken Livers with Fresh Figs* / 156

*Chicken Blanquette (Chicken and Gravy)* / 158

*Rustic Beef and Pork Meatloaf* / 160

*Pork Shoulder Picnic Roast* / 162

*Grilled Lamb Chops* / 164

*Lavender and Honey Pork Medallions* / 166

*Meatballs with Nomato Sauce* / 168

# Sage Roast Chicken

*This is the simplest way to prepare chicken: roast until crisp, then combine with fruit and herbs to garnish! What's not to love?*

Prep time: 10 minutes  ❧  Cook time: 1 hour 30 minutes  ❧  Yield: 4–5 servings

## INGREDIENTS

*1 tablespoon extra-virgin olive oil + extra for greasing the dish*

*1 whole chicken (about 4 pounds), giblets removed*

*Handful fresh sage leaves (about 5–6 leaves) + extra for garnish*

*1 tablespoon dried sage*

*½ teaspoon fine sea salt*

*Orange slices, for garnish*

## INSTRUCTIONS

1. Heat oven to 350° F. Set the rack in the middle of the oven. Grease the bottom of a baking dish with olive oil.

2. Place chicken, breast up, in the baking dish and stuff cavity with sage leaves.

3. Massage chicken skin with olive oil, then season with sea salt and dried sage.

4. Roast, basting occasionally, until juices run clear, about 90 minutes.

5. Let chicken rest 10 minutes before carving. Serve with a garnish of sage leaves and orange slices.

SERVE WITH: *No Nightshade Ratatouille (page 128), Oven-Roasted Fennel and Garlic (page 130), Creamy Broccoli Mash (page 132), Roasted Vegetable Medley (page 134), Balsamic Spaghetti Squash (page 136), Celeriac Remoulade (page 138), Zingy Beet and Carrot Salad (page 140), Brussels Sprout Hash (page 142), Cauliflower Salad with Scallions (page 144), or Pan-Fried Sweet Potatoes with Sage (page 146).*

# Herbed Roast Lamb

*I encourage you to carve this roast at the table. The ritual adds to the pleasure taken in the meal and everyone around the table will enjoy the ceremony. This is definitely a holiday or celebration dish at our house.*

Prep time: 20 minutes  ❧  Cook time: 1 hour 30 minutes  ❧  Yield: 6–8 servings

## INGREDIENTS

2 tablespoons extra-virgin olive oil + extra for greasing the pan

1 head garlic

1 boneless leg of lamb (about 4–5 pounds)

¾ pound shallots, skin on

2 tablespoons Herbes de Provence (page 232)

1 teaspoon fine sea salt

NOTE: *To deglaze, add ⅓ cup water or broth to pan drippings. Cook for a few minutes on top of the stove over medium–high heat, scraping the bottom of the pan to incorporate drippings and loosen any browned bits.*

SERVE WITH: *No Nightshade Ratatouille (page 128), Oven-Roasted Fennel and Garlic (page 130), Creamy Broccoli Mash (page 132), Roasted Vegetable Medley (page 134), Balsamic Spaghetti Squash (page 136), Brussels Sprout Hash (page 142), Cauliflower Salad with Scallions (page 144), or Pan-Fried Sweet Potatoes with Sage (page 146).*

## INSTRUCTIONS

1. Heat oven to 325° F. Set the rack in the middle of the oven. Grease the bottom of a roasting pan with olive oil.

2. Peel garlic and cut each clove into almond-shaped slivers.

3. With a paring knife, carefully make about a dozen small cuts in the surface of the meat, about ½-inch deep. Insert garlic shards into these small cuts and push down into the meat.

4. Put lamb in the roasting pan and scatter shallots around meat.

5. Drizzle remaining olive oil over meat, season with herbes de Provence and sea salt.

6. Roast for 20 minutes per pound, about 90 minutes total, or to an internal temperature of 145° F for medium-rare. Baste lamb a couple of times while cooking.

7. Remove lamb from the roasting pan and allow meat to rest for 10 minutes before carving.

8. If meat is trussed, now is the time to discard any binding.

9. Deglaze the pan if desired. To serve, spoon glaze over lamb roast.

# Tarragon Provençal Chicken

*All the flavors of French Provençal cuisine are present in this casserole. If you are lucky and have any left over, it will taste even better the next day!*

Prep time: 15 minutes  ✤  Cook time: 1 hour 15 minutes  ✤  Yield: 4–5 servings

## INGREDIENTS

*1 tablespoon extra-virgin olive oil + extra for greasing the dish*

*2 pounds chicken thighs and/or drumsticks*

*¾ teaspoon fine sea salt*

*1 small red onion (about ⅓ pound), thinly sliced*

*¾ cup green olives, pitted*

*1 lemon, cut into 8 wedges*

*3 cloves garlic, minced*

*1 cup full fat coconut milk*

*2 teaspoons dried tarragon*

## INSTRUCTIONS

1. Heat oven to 350° F. Set the rack in the middle of the oven. Grease the bottom of a baking dish with olive oil.

2. Arrange chicken pieces in the bottom of the baking dish in a single layer. Drizzle with olive oil and season with sea salt.

3. Arrange onion, olives, lemon, and garlic around chicken. Pour coconut milk over all ingredients and sprinkle with tarragon.

4. Bake until chicken is cooked through, about 60 to 75 minutes. Discard lemon before serving. Check seasoning and adjust salt to taste.

SERVE WITH: *Oven-Roasted Fennel and Garlic (page 130), Creamy Broccoli Mash (page 132), Roasted Vegetable Medley (page 134), or Cauliflower Salad with Scallions (page 144).*

# Chicken Livers with Fresh Figs

*Chicken livers are inexpensive and a nutritional powerhouse. You can enjoy them in the form of my tasty Creamy Liver Pâté (page 66), or as here, partnered with fresh figs. This wonderful combination of tastes and textures, with a rich sweet-and-sour sauce, will have you coming back for more.*

Prep time: 10 minutes ❧ Cook time: 8 minutes ❧ Yield: 4 servings

## INGREDIENTS

*5 fresh figs*

*1 pound chicken livers*

*1 tablespoon balsamic vinegar*

*½ tablespoon Herbes de Provence (page 232)*

*½ teaspoon fine sea salt*

*3 tablespoons extra-virgin olive oil*

*Chopped fresh thyme, for garnish*

## INSTRUCTIONS

1. Wash figs. Slice off tops and quarter. Set aside.

2. Rinse livers thoroughly and pat dry. With a sharp knife, trim any sinew and cut each liver into bite size pieces.

3. In a bowl, combine livers, vinegar, herbes de Provence, and sea salt. Mix well.

4. In a large skillet, heat olive oil over medium-low heat and cook livers for 8 to 10 minutes, stirring occasionally. Liver is cooked when just pink inside.

5. Turn off heat and add figs. Mix gently to coat figs with sauce, then cover and let stand for five minutes before serving.

6. Garnish with fresh thyme.

NOTE: *Liver is best eaten fresh. If figs are not in season, try replacing with grapes.*

SERVE WITH: *No Nightshade Ratatouille (page 128), Roasted Vegetable Medley (page 134), Balsamic Spaghetti Squash (page 136), Zingy Beet and Carrot Salad (page 140), or Pan-Fried Sweet Potatoes with Sage (page 146).*

# Chicken Blanquette (Chicken and Gravy)

*This is an easy, almost one-pot meal that everyone enjoys at my house. Succulent chicken pieces, earthy mushrooms, sweet carrots, and savory onions partner beautifully to create a mouthwatering dish. This is my own dairy-free version.*

Prep time: 15 minutes  ❧  Cook time: 50 minutes  ❧  Yield: 4 servings

## INGREDIENTS

3 tablespoons extra-virgin olive oil

3 medium carrots (about ½ pound), peeled and cut into ¼-inch slices

1 medium yellow onion (about ½ pound), peeled and roughly chopped

½ pound white mushrooms, quartered

3 boneless, skinless chicken breasts (about 1¾ pounds), cut into 1-inch pieces

2 cups Chicken Bone Broth (page 234)

1 tablespoon dried thyme

2 bay leaves

1 teaspoon fine sea salt, divided

3½ tablespoons arrowroot flour

1½ tablespoons lemon juice

---

SERVE WITH: *No Nightshade Ratatouille (page 128), Oven-Roasted Fennel and Garlic (page 130), Roasted Vegetable Medley (page 134), Cauliflower Salad with Scallions (page 144), or Pan-Fried Sweet Potatoes with Sage (page 146).*

## INSTRUCTIONS

1. In a large skillet, heat olive oil over medium heat. Add carrots and onion. Cover and cook for five minutes.

2. Add mushrooms and cook, covered, for another five minutes.

3. Add chicken, chicken broth, thyme, bay leaves, and ¾ teaspoon sea salt. Cover and cook, stirring occasionally, until vegetables are tender, about 30 minutes. If dish starts boiling too fast, reduce heat to medium–low.

4. Transfer chicken and vegetables to a serving dish with a slotted spoon. Discard bay leaves and reserve cooking liquid.

5. In a small dish, combine arrowroot flour with ½ cup of cooking liquid, making sure flour is completely dissolved and there are no lumps. Set aside.

6. Pour remaining cooking liquid into a saucepan. Add lemon juice, remaining ¼ teaspoon sea salt, and bring to a low boil.

7. Add arrowroot mixture to hot broth and whisk vigorously until sauce thickens, about 15 seconds. Check seasoning and adjust salt to taste.

8. Pour sauce over chicken and vegetables. Serve hot.

# Rustic Beef and Pork Meatloaf

*This recipe is a big hit with kids—both young and old! And I love that you can pair it with pretty much any kind of vegetable. I recommend doubling, or even tripling, the quantities to prepare extra loaves. They freeze extremely well and will make your life easier when things get busy around the house.*

Prep time: 15 minutes  ❧  Cook time: 75 minutes  ❧  Yield: 5–6 servings

## INGREDIENTS

*Extra-virgin olive oil for greasing the pan*

*1 pound ground beef*

*1 pound ground pork*

*4 slices bacon, cut into ¼-inch strips*

*1 small yellow onion (about ⅓ pound), finely chopped*

*1 small green apple, finely chopped*

*2 tablespoons dried sage*

*1½ teaspoons fine sea salt*

## INSTRUCTIONS

1. Heat oven to 350° F. Set the rack in the middle of the oven. Grease a loaf pan (8 ½" x 4 ½") with olive oil.

2. In a large bowl, combine all ingredients, mixing well with your hands. Press meat mixture evenly into the loaf pan.

3. Bake until meatloaf starts to pull away from the sides of the pan or reaches an internal temperature of 150° F, about 75 minutes. Serve hot.

SERVE WITH: *No Nightshade Ratatouille (page 128), Oven-Roasted Fennel and Garlic (page 130), Creamy Broccoli Mash (page 132), Roasted Vegetable Medley (page 134), Balsamic Spaghetti Squash (page 136), Zingy Beet and Carrot Salad (page 140), Brussels Sprout Hash (page 142), Cauliflower Salad with Scallions (page 144), or Pan-Fried Sweet Potatoes with Sage (page 146).*

# Pork Shoulder Picnic Roast

*Love roast pork, but wary of attempting it? Here is a simple path to delectable, perfect roast pork—success guaranteed every time!*

Prep time: 5 minutes ❧ Cook time: 1 hour 30 minutes ❧ Yield: 5–6 servings

## INGREDIENTS

*1 tablespoon extra-virgin olive oil + extra for greasing the pan*

*4 sprigs fresh rosemary*

*4 sprigs fresh thyme*

*1 pork shoulder, picnic-style (about 2-2½ pounds)*

*1 teaspoon fine sea salt*

---

NOTE: *To deglaze, add ⅓ cup water or broth to pan drippings. Cook for a few minutes on top of the stove over medium–high heat, scraping the bottom of the pan to incorporate drippings and loosen any browned bits.*

## INSTRUCTIONS

1. Heat oven to 350° F. Set the rack in the middle of the oven. Grease the bottom of a roasting pan with olive oil.

2. Line the roasting pan with rosemary and thyme. Place roast on top. Season with one tablespoon olive oil and sea salt.

3. Roast until juices run clear, basting occasionally, about 90 minutes.

4. Allow meat to rest for 10 minutes before carving.

5. While meat is resting, deglaze the pan. To serve, spoon glaze over pork roast.

---

SERVE WITH: *No Nightshade Ratatouille (page 128), Oven-Roasted Fennel and Garlic (page 130), Creamy Broccoli Mash (page 132), Roasted Vegetable Medley (page 134), Balsamic Spaghetti Squash (page 136), Celeriac Remoulade (page 138), Zingy Beet and Carrot Salad (page 140), Brussels Sprout Hash (page 142), Cauliflower Salad with Scallions (page 144), or Pan-Fried Sweet Potatoes with Sage (page 146).*

# Grilled Lamb Chops

*These lamb cutlets taste ten times better if you eat them with your fingers! They should be neither rare nor well done—rather, just right. Thick pieces of meat give the best results.*

Prep time: 10 minutes + marinade ❧ Cook time: 8 minutes ❧ Yield: 4 servings

## INGREDIENTS

2 tablespoons minced fresh rosemary

2 tablespoons minced fresh thyme

2 cloves garlic, minced

5 tablespoons extra-virgin olive oil

8 (1-inch thick) lamb chops (about 1½ pounds), frenched

Fine sea salt

\* Special equipment needed: mortar and pestle or food processor

## INSTRUCTIONS

1. With a mortar and pestle (or food processor), grind rosemary, thyme, garlic, and olive oil to a paste.

2. Transfer paste to a large glass or ceramic dish. Add lamb chops to marinade, turning to coat. Cover and marinate in the refrigerator for at least two hours, turning once or twice.

3. At least one hour before cooking, remove lamb from the refrigerator. Salt both sides of each chop.

4. Heat barbecue to medium and grill chops for three to four minutes per side. Alternatively, broil chops for about four minutes per side.

SERVE WITH: *No Nightshade Ratatouille (page 128), Oven-Roasted Fennel and Garlic (page 130), Creamy Broccoli Mash (page 132), Roasted Vegetable Medley (page 134), Balsamic Spaghetti Squash (page 136), Cauliflower Salad with Scallions (page 144), Pan-Fried Sweet Potatoes with Sage (page 146).*

# Lavender and Honey Pork Medallions

*The lavender and honey marinade transforms this simple cut of meat into a truly mouth-watering meal. You won't want to prepare your pork medallions any other way in the future! This recipe works equally well with pork chops.*

Prep time: 5 minutes + marinade  ❦  Cook time: 20 minutes  ❦  Yield: 4 servings

## INGREDIENTS

½ tablespoon lavender flowers

¼ teaspoon fine sea salt

6 tablespoons extra-virgin olive oil

2 tablespoons honey

1 tablespoon apple cider vinegar

4 pork medallions (about 1¼ pounds)

NOTE: *To deglaze, add ⅓ cup water or broth to pan drippings. Cook for a few minutes on top of the stove over medium–high heat, scraping the bottom of the pan to incorporate drippings and loosen any browned bits.*

## INSTRUCTIONS

1. Combine lavender, sea salt, olive oil, honey, and vinegar in a glass or ceramic dish. Add pork medallions to marinade, turning to coat.

2. Cover and marinate in the refrigerator for at least two hours, turning once or twice.

3. Heat oven to 350° F. Set the rack in the middle of the oven.

4. Remove meat from the refrigerator and place into a roasting pan. Pour marinade over meat.

5. Bake until meat is slightly pink inside and juices run clear, about 20 minutes. Baste a couple of times during baking.

6. Remove medallions from the roasting pan and if desired, deglaze the pan.

7. To serve, spoon glaze over pork medallions.

SERVE WITH: *No Nightshade Ratatouille (page 128), Roasted Vegetable Medley (page 134), Balsamic Spaghetti Squash (page 136), Zingy Beet and Carrot Salad (page 140), or Pan-Fried Sweet Potatoes with Sage (page 146).*

# Meatballs with Nomato Sauce

*You can still enjoy the traditional favorite of meatballs and sauce even if you have to avoid tomatoes! This clever "Nomato" sauce will make you believe you are eating the real deal. Definitely a favorite with the kids!*

Prep time: 10 minutes ❧ Cook time: 35 minutes ❧ Yield: 12 meatballs (4 servings)

## INGREDIENTS

*Extra-virgin olive oil for greasing the dish*

*1 pound ground beef*

*1 pound ground bison*

*1 can (4-ounce) mushrooms, drained (about ¾ cup)*

*¼ cup finely chopped fresh parsley + extra for garnish*

*2 cloves garlic, minced*

*1½ teaspoons fine sea salt*

*1 Nomato Sauce (page 228)*

NOTE: *Ground beef, lamb, or pork can be substituted for the bison. Meatballs also freeze well.*

## INSTRUCTIONS

1. Heat oven to 350° F. Set the rack in the middle of the oven. Grease the bottom of a baking dish with olive oil.

2. Using your hands, combine meat, mushrooms, parsley, garlic, and sea salt in a large bowl.

3. Continuing to use your hands, scoop out ⅓-cup-sized portions of meat mixture and form into meatballs.

4. Place meatballs in the baking dish. Bake until meat is browned and cooked through, about 35 minutes.

5. Serve meatballs with a generous dollop of Nomato sauce and a garnish of fresh parsley.

SERVE WITH: *Dandelion Leaf Salad (page 86), Crunchy Red Cabbage and Kale Salad (page 90), No Nightshade Ratatouille (page 128), Creamy Broccoli Mash (page 132), Roasted Vegetable Medley (page 134), Balsamic Spaghetti Squash (page 136), Brussels Sprout Hash (page 142), Cauliflower Salad with Scallions (page 144), or Pan-Fried Sweet Potatoes with Sage (page 146).*

No.6
SEAFOOD

# Fisherman Soup

*This hearty soup, with its variety of tastes and aromas, is a full meal in itself requiring no more than a green salad as an accompaniment.*

Prep time: 15 minutes ❧ Cook time: 35 minutes ❧ Yield: 3½ quarts / 7 (16-ounce) servings

## INGREDIENTS

6 tablespoons extra-virgin olive oil, divided

1 medium yellow onion (about ½ pound), peeled and chopped

1 large white sweet potato (about 1 pound), peeled and cut into ½-inch pieces

2 bay leaves

2 sprigs fresh thyme

2 teaspoons fine sea salt

2 quarts Fish Bone Broth (page 236)

1 large leek (about ¾ pound), washed and thinly sliced

1 pound fresh cod fillet, cut into 1-inch pieces

1 pound fresh salmon fillet, cut into 1-inch pieces

½ pound smoked salmon, sliced into ¼-inch strips

Minced fresh thyme, for garnish

## INSTRUCTIONS

1. Heat three tablespoons olive oil in a large stockpot. Add onion and sauté over medium–high heat, stirring frequently, until translucent, about five minutes.

2. Add sweet potatoes, bay leaves, thyme, sea salt, and fish broth. Bring to a low boil and cook, covered, until vegetables are tender, about 15 to 20 minutes.

3. While vegetables are cooking, heat remaining three tablespoons olive oil in a large skillet. Add leeks and cook, uncovered, until crisp-tender, about 8 to 10 minutes.

4. Remove soup from heat. Discard bay leaves and thyme. Mix thoroughly with an immersion blender until smooth.

5. Return to heat and bring back to a boil. Add fresh salmon and cod. Cook, covered, until fish is cooked through, about five minutes.

6. Turn off heat. Add leeks and smoked salmon. Check seasoning and adjust salt to taste. Serve hot with a garnish of fresh thyme.

NOTE: *This soup is not suitable for freezing.*

# Baked Cod with Black Olive Tapenade

*In this dish, the cod cooks quickly while the tapenade crust adds the rich Provençal flavors of garlic and olives.*

Prep time: 10 minutes  ❧  Cook time: 20 minutes  ❧  Yield: 4 servings

## INGREDIENTS

*1 tablespoon extra-virgin olive oil*

*4 fresh cod fillets (6 ounces each)*

*Black Olive Tapenade (page 226)*

*1 lemon, sliced*

## INSTRUCTIONS

1. Heat oven to 350° F. Set the rack in the middle of the oven. Grease the bottom of a baking dish with olive oil.

2. Place fish in the baking dish and spread 1½ tablespoons tapenade over each fillet.

3. Bake until flesh flakes easily when tested with a fork, about 15 to 20 minutes.

4. Garnish with lemon slices and serve immediately.

NOTE: *There is no need to salt the fish as the tapenade will bring enough seasoning to the dish.*

SERVE WITH: *Dandelion Leaf Salad (page 86), No Nightshade Ratatouille (page 128), Oven-Roasted Fennel and Garlic (page 130), Creamy Broccoli Mash (page 132), Celeriac Remoulade (page 138), or Cauliflower Salad with Scallions (page 144).*

# Oven-Baked Turmeric Tilapia

*Turmeric is a powerful anti-inflammatory; the more of it you can consume, the better. Its yellow-gold color is reminiscent of curry, but milder. This tasty dish is an easy way to add more turmeric to your diet.*

Prep time: 10 minutes + marinade  &  Cook time: 20 minutes  &  Yield: 4 servings

## INGREDIENTS

4 fresh tilapia fillets (6 ounces each)

1 cup chopped scallions

½ cup finely chopped yellow onion

4 tablespoons extra-virgin olive oil

3 tablespoons lemon juice

1 teaspoon turmeric

¼ teaspoon fine sea salt

## INSTRUCTIONS

1. Rinse tilapia fillets and pat dry.

2. In a large glass or ceramic dish, combine scallions, onion, olive oil, lemon juice, turmeric, and sea salt. Add fish to marinade, ensuring each fillet is completely coated.

3. Cover and marinate in the refrigerator for about one hour, turning once or twice.

4. Heat oven to 350° F. Set the rack in the middle of the oven.

5. Transfer fish to a baking dish. Pour marinade over fish.

6. Bake until fish flakes easily when tested with a fork, about 20 minutes. Serve immediately.

SERVE WITH: *Kale and Ginger Salad (page 98), Oven-Roasted Fennel and Garlic (page 130), Creamy Broccoli Mash (page 132), Roasted Vegetable Medley (page 134), or Cauliflower Salad with Scallions (page 144).*

# Grilled Shrimp with Aïoli

*A simple dish that can be served as a main course or as finger-food at your next party!*

Prep time: 10 minutes ❦ Cook time: 4 minutes ❦ Yield: 4 servings

## INGREDIENTS

16 extra-large fresh shrimp (about ¾ pound), deveined and peeled, with tails on

2 tablespoons extra-virgin olive oil

1 teaspoon dried thyme

⅛ teaspoon fine sea salt

1 cup Aïoli (page 240)

## INSTRUCTIONS

1. Set the oven broiler to high. Set the rack five inches below heating element.

2. Rinse shrimp and pat dry.

3. Combine shrimp, olive oil, thyme, and sea salt in a bowl. Mix well.

4. Arrange shrimp in a single layer on a baking sheet and broil until shrimp turn pink, about two minutes each side.

5. Serve shrimp hot or cold with aïoli.

NOTE: *These shrimp also taste great grilled.*

SERVE WITH: *Shrimp and Citrus Salad (page 92), No Nightshade Ratatouille (page 128), Celeriac Remoulade (page 138), Zingy Beet and Carrot Salad (page 140), or Cauliflower Salad with Scallions (page 144).*

# Brandade Express with Cauliflower Purée

*Traditionally prepared with salt cod, which needs to be soaked for at least 24 hours, brandade is an excellent example of French comfort food. I prefer this version using fresh cod because it is ready in less than 30 minutes, which makes it doable for a weeknight dinner. I like to mix everything together on my plate before eating; it tastes better that way!*

---

Prep time: 10 minutes  ❧  Cook time: 20 minutes  ❧  Yield: 4 servings

---

## INGREDIENTS

2 pounds cauliflower florets
(1 large cauliflower)

3 tablespoons extra-virgin olive oil +
extra for garnish

1½ pounds fresh cod fillet, skinned

1 teaspoon fine sea salt, divided

¼ cup full fat coconut milk

2 cloves garlic, minced

Minced fresh parsley, for garnish

* Special equipment needed: blender or
food processor

## INSTRUCTIONS

1. Steam cauliflower until tender, about 20 minutes.

2. Heat olive oil in a large skillet over medium heat. Place cod fillets into the hot skillet, season with ½ teaspoon sea salt and cook, covered, for about 10 to 12 minutes. Fish should be firm, white, and flake off easily into large chunks when tested with a fork. Set aside and keep warm.

3. Transfer steamed cauliflower to a blender or food processor. Add coconut milk, garlic, and remaining ½ teaspoon sea salt. Process until smooth and creamy. Check seasoning and adjust salt to taste.

4. To serve, divide cauliflower purée between four plates and top with fish. You may also mix fish and cauliflower together before serving. Garnish with fresh parsley and a drizzle of olive oil.

---

NOTE: *For my tutorial on steaming, refer to page 58.*

# Pan-Seared Salmon with Sweet and Sour Vegetables

*This well-balanced combination of vegetables, fruit, and apple cider vinegar will definitely surprise and delight your palate!*

Prep time: 15 minutes ❧ Cook time: 40 minutes ❧ Yield: 4 servings

## INGREDIENTS

6 tablespoons extra-virgin olive oil, divided

1 large yellow onion (about ¾ pound), thinly sliced

2 large carrots (about ½ pound), thinly sliced

1 medium red apple, finely diced

3 cloves garlic, minced

1 teaspoon minced fresh rosemary

¼ teaspoon fine sea salt, divided

Zest of one lemon

¼ cup full fat coconut milk

1 tablespoon apple cider vinegar

4 fresh salmon fillets (4 to 6 ounces each), skin on

Minced fresh parsley and lemon slices, for garnish

## INSTRUCTIONS

1. Heat three tablespoons olive oil in a large skillet over medium heat. Add onion and sauté until translucent, about five minutes.

2. Add carrots and apple. Sauté until crisp-tender, stirring frequently, about five minutes.

3. Add garlic, rosemary, ⅛ teaspoon sea salt, lemon zest, coconut milk, and vinegar. Mix well. Reduce heat to medium-low, and cook, covered, until vegetables are tender, about 10 minutes.

4. Transfer cooked vegetables to a plate and keep warm.

5. In the same skillet, heat remaining three tablespoons olive oil over medium-low heat. Add salmon fillets, skin side down. Sprinkle with remaining ⅛ teaspoon sea salt and cook, covered, until fish flakes easily when tested with a fork, about 10 minutes.

6. Check seasoning and adjust salt to taste. Serve hot with a garnish of fresh parsley and lemon slices.

SERVE WITH: *Colorful, Fruity Fennel Salad (page 88), No Nightshade Ratatouille (page 128), Zingy Beet and Carrot Salad (page 140), Cauliflower Salad with Scallions (page 144), or Pan-Fried Sweet Potatoes with Sage (page 146).*

# Oven-Baked Snapper with Fennel

*A large fish baked whole and presented at the table in its baking dish is always impressive. I like to serve this for special occasions or when we have guests coming over. Such a dish really needs no sauce! Olive oil and lemon slices are all you need.*

Prep time: 10 minutes  ❦  Cook time: 30 minutes  ❦  Yield: 4 servings

## INGREDIENTS

¼ cup extra-virgin olive oil + extra for greasing the dish

1 whole fresh snapper, or other fish of choice (about 2 pounds), gutted

Handful fresh fennel fronds + extra, minced, for garnish

1 tablespoon lemon juice

½ teaspoon fine sea salt

1 lemon, sliced

## INSTRUCTIONS

1. Heat oven to 350° F. Set the rack in the middle of the oven. Grease the bottom of a baking dish with olive oil.

2. Rinse fish and pat dry. Score fish on each side with a sharp knife, making two or three shallow cuts crosswise. Place fish in the baking dish.

3. Stuff fennel stalks into body and head cavity of fish.

4. Drizzle fish with olive oil, both inside and out. Splash with lemon juice and season with sea salt. Arrange lemon slices along the length of fish.

5. Bake, basting a couple of times, until fish flakes easily when tested with a fork, about 25 to 30 minutes. (*See special note below.*)

6. Serve with a garnish of minced fennel

NOTE: *The cooking time for a whole fish is judged by the fish's back at its thickest point, counting about 10 minutes per inch.*

SERVE WITH: *Colorful, Fruity Fennel Salad (page 88), Oven-Roasted Fennel and Garlic (page 130), Creamy Broccoli Mash (page 132), Roasted Vegetable Medley (page 134), or Celeriac Remoulade (page 138).*

# Seared Scallops with Persillade

*A very simple dish, yet bursting with flavor, Provençal persillade is made of minced garlic and parsley. The trick to mincing parsley without making a mess is that the leaves must be absolutely dry! A very sharp kitchen knife also helps a lot, but mind those fingers.*

Prep time: 10 minutes ⁘ Cook time: 4 minutes ⁘ Yield: 4 servings

## INGREDIENTS

*16 fresh medium sea scallops (about 1½ pounds)*

*4 tablespoons extra-virgin olive oil*

*2 cloves garlic, minced*

*4 tablespoons minced fresh parsley*

*Juice of half a lemon*

*Fine sea salt*

## INSTRUCTIONS

1. Rinse sea scallops, pat dry, and season with sea salt on each side.

2. In a large skillet, heat olive oil over medium-high heat. Add scallops to the skillet, ensuring they don't touch each other (you might have to do this in two batches) and sauté, one and a half to two minutes per side. Scallops are done when they have a golden crust while still being translucent in the center.

3. Add parsley and garlic to the pan. Drizzle with lemon juice and toss for a few seconds to coat scallops evenly. Serve immediately.

SERVE WITH: *Endive, Pear, and Spinach Salad (page 94), No Nightshade Ratatouille (page 128), Oven-Roasted Fennel and Garlic (page 130), or Creamy Broccoli Mash (page 132).*

# Baked Salmon with Lemon and Dill Sauce

*I particularly love this preparation for salmon. I find the combination of lemon and fresh dill in the sauce to be so elegant and refined, making it perfect for special occasions and celebrations. The best part though? How fast it all comes together!*

Prep time: 15 minutes ❧ Cook time: 18 minutes ❧ Yield: 2–3 servings

## INGREDIENTS

*1 teaspoon extra-virgin olive oil + extra for greasing the dish*

*1 pound fresh salmon fillets*

*¼ teaspoon fine sea salt + extra for the sauce*

*1 cup coconut cream (see special note below)*

*2 tablespoons minced fresh dill + extra for garnish*

*2 teaspoons lemon juice*

*1 tablespoon arrowroot flour*

*1 lemon, sliced*

NOTE: *Coconut cream can be scooped off the top of a can of full fat coconut milk, which has been refrigerated for at least 24 hours (the cream separates from the water at cold temperatures). To make sure you have enough cream for the recipe, I recommend chilling at least two cans. Save the leftover coconut water, if there is any, for a smoothie (page 216).*

## INSTRUCTIONS

1. Heat oven to 350° F. Set the rack in the middle of the oven. Grease the bottom of a baking dish with olive oil.

2. Place salmon in the dish, skin side down, rub with olive oil and season with sea salt. Bake for 15 to 18 minutes. Fish is done when flesh just starts to flake when tested with a fork.

3. In a saucepan, melt coconut cream over medium heat for a couple of minutes. Add dill, pinch sea salt, and lemon juice. Stir.

4. In a small dish, measure ¼ cup coconut mixture from the saucepan. Add arrowroot flour. Stir, making sure flour is completely dissolved and there are no lumps. Set aside.

5. Turn up heat to medium–high and bring coconut mixture to a low boil. Add arrowroot mixture and whisk vigorously until sauce thickens, about 20 seconds. Check seasoning and adjust salt to taste.

6. To serve, pour sauce over hot fish and garnish with fresh dill and lemon slices.

SERVE WITH: *Colorful, Fruity Fennel Salad (page 88), Creamy Broccoli Mash (page 132), Celeriac Remoulade (page 138), or Cauliflower Salad with Scallions (page 144).*

# Bouillabaisse-Inspired Seafood Stew

*The original bouillabaisse was prepared with unsold fish from the day's catch and infused with wild herbs. Today, there are as many versions as there are fish in the sea. This is my own personal version, nutrient-dense and full of vegetables to form a complete, balanced meal.*

Prep time: 20 minutes ❧ Cook time: 20 minutes ❧ Yield: 4–6 servings

## INGREDIENTS

4 tablespoons extra-virgin olive oil

1½ cups thinly sliced fennel

1½ cups thinly sliced celery

1½ cups thinly sliced yellow onion

4 cloves garlic, minced

2 quarts Fish Bone Broth (page 236), divided

3 sprigs fresh thyme

1 bay leaf

2 teaspoons fine sea salt

1 pound fresh calamari tubes, sliced into ½-inch rings

1 pound fresh mussels

1 pound fresh shrimp

Minced fresh parsley, for garnish

## INSTRUCTIONS

1. In a large skillet, heat olive oil over medium heat. Add fennel, celery, onion, garlic, and ¼ cup fish broth. Bring to a simmer. Cover and cook until tender, but not caramelized, stirring occasionally, about 12 to 15 minutes.

2. In a large stockpot, add remaining fish broth, thyme, bay leaf, and sea salt. Bring to a boil. Add calamari, mussels, and shrimp. Cook until mussels open and shrimp turn pink, about four minutes.

3. Remove from heat. Add cooked vegetables to soup and let flavors imbue, about 10 minutes.

4. Serve hot with a garnish of fresh parsley.

NOTE: *With a traditional, rustic French bouillabaisse, the shellfish is served in its shell. There is no choice with the mussels, but certainly, if you prefer, peel the shrimp before cooking.*

No. 7
DESSERTS
& DRINKS

# French Crèpes

*In Paris, there are crèpe-stands everywhere. They are an integral part of French life, which is why I was inspired to create an AIP-friendly version. This recipe can be a little bit fiddly the first time around. AIP batters are tricky, but I promise you'll be so happy once you master it. Impress your family and friends with your mad flipping skills! Or choose the safer route and simply use a spatula. These crèpes can be enjoyed with the sweet or savory topping of your choice. The combinations are endless!*

Prep time: 10 minutes + 15 minutes wait time  ❧  Cook time: 35 minutes  ❧  Yield: 8 crèpes

## INGREDIENTS

½ cup (3 ounces) cassava flour

¼ cup (1 ounce) tigernut flour

3 tablespoons coconut flour

¼ teaspoon baking soda

Pinch fine sea salt

1¼ cups (10 ounces) full fat coconut milk

1 cup (8½ ounces) water

1 tablespoon maple syrup

Triple Berry Sauce (page 214)

Whipped Cream (page 212)

* An 8-inch nonstick skillet yields 8 crèpes. Use a ⅓ cup measure to scoop batter. A 10-inch nonstick skillet yields 5 crèpes. Use a ½ cup measure to pour batter.

NOTE: *If freezing crèpes, layer parchment paper in between each crèpe and seal in an airtight container.*

## INSTRUCTIONS

1. Combine the first eight ingredients in a large bowl and mix with a whisk or an immersion blender to obtain a smooth batter. Let batter rest for 15 minutes at room temperature.

2. Heat an 8-inch nonstick skillet over medium–high heat. Add ⅓ cup batter and gently tilt the skillet to spread batter evenly. Batter should be sizzling slightly and forming small bubbles on the surface. Adjust the temperature if needed.

3. Cook until bottom of crèpe is golden and the top looks "dry," about three minutes.

4. Carefully flip crèpe over with a wide spatula and cook for an additional one and a half minutes.

5. Serve with triple berry sauce and a generous dollop of whipped cream!

### TROUBLESHOOTING

➤ If batter is too loose (and the crèpes are breaking when you flip them), add cassava flour, one tablespoon at a time.

➤ If batter is too thick, add water, one tablespoon at a time.

# Layered Raspberry Crèpe Cake

*I love to prepare this cake for birthdays and very special occasions. It is light, refreshing, and definitely a show-stopper! If you can prepare the ingredients one or two days in advance, putting this cake together at the last minute is fairly easy and takes no time at all. I have tried many different combinations (large crèpes, small crèpes, high stacks, low stacks) and I find that using eight to ten 8-inch crèpes works best.*

Prep time: 35 minutes ❧ Cook time: 65 minutes ❧ Yield: 8 servings

### INGREDIENTS

*8 to 10 (8-inch) French Crèpes (page 194)*

*2 batches Raspberry Whipped Cream (page 212)*

*Fresh raspberries and blueberries, for garnish*

*1 batch Triple Berry Sauce (page 214)*

### INSTRUCTIONS

1. Starting with a crèpe at the bottom, alternate one crèpe, followed by a thin layer of raspberry whipped cream. Repeat until all crèpes are used.

2. Top finished cake with a smooth layer of raspberry whipped cream. Garnish with fresh raspberries and blueberries.

3. Serve with a generous dollop of triple berry sauce and more whipped cream!

NOTE: *The crèpes and berry sauce can be prepared two days in advance. The raspberry whipped cream may be prepared the day before. Assemble the cake the day you serve it.*

# Sophie's Signature Pear Cake

*This pear cake is my pride and joy! It took many attempts to perfect the recipe and my poor husband and kids had to taste many versions, but they rose to the task and thanks to their dedication, you can also enjoy a tasty pear cake that will knock your socks off! I like to pair it with a warm cup of Lavender-Rose Tea (page 220).*

Prep time: 20 minutes  🌿  Cook time: 22 minutes  🌿  Yield: 8 servings

## INGREDIENTS

*Extra-virgin olive oil for greasing the dish*

*1 cup (3.6 ounces) tigernut flour*

*½ cup (2 ounces) arrowroot flour*

*3 tablespoons coconut flour*

*¾ teaspoon baking soda*

*¼ teaspoon fine sea salt*

*½ cup (3.2 ounces) palm shortening, melted*

*⅓ cup (3 ounces) unsweetened applesauce*

*¼ cup (3 ounces) maple syrup*

*2 teaspoons vanilla extract (see special note below)*

*2 tablespoons gelatin powder*

*2 pears, just ripe*

---

NOTE: *The alcohol present in the vanilla extract will be cooked off during baking. You may substitute with 1 teaspoon of vanilla powder, if desired.*

## INSTRUCTIONS

1. Heat oven to 350° F. Set the rack in the middle of the oven. Lightly grease the bottom of a glass or ceramic pie dish (9½-inch diameter) with olive oil.

2. In a large bowl, combine tigernut flour, arrowroot flour, coconut flour, baking soda, and sea salt. Mix well.

3. In a separate bowl, mix palm shortening, applesauce, maple syrup, and vanilla extract. Stir well.

4. Sprinkle gelatin powder over palm shortening mixture and whisk vigorously until well blended.

5. Pour liquid mixture into dry ingredients and mix well with a spatula, ensuring there are no lumps.

6. Spread dough evenly into the baking dish. (The mixture is sticky so I find it easier to use my fingers.)

7. Peel and core pears. Slice each pear lengthwise into eight pieces.

8. Arrange pear slices on top of dough in a pinwheel fashion, pressing down gently with your fingers.

9. Bake until cake is golden brown and a toothpick inserted near the center comes out clean, about 22 to 25 minutes.

10. Allow cake to cool completely before serving—this is the hard part!

# Honey-Lavender Roasted Peaches

*This is a lovely dessert and couldn't be simpler to prepare. The gentle fragrance of lavender is subtle and inviting.*

Prep time: 10 minutes ❦ Cook time: 10 minutes ❦ Yield: 4 servings

## INGREDIENTS

4 medium peaches, ripe but firm

4 tablespoons coconut oil

1½ tablespoons honey

½ teaspoon dried lavender flowers

## INSTRUCTIONS

1. Peel peaches and cut into eight crescents.

2. In a large skillet over medium heat, heat coconut oil, honey, and lavender for a couple of minutes until blended.

3. Add peaches and stir, ensuring fruit is well coated with syrup.

4. Cover and cook for ten minutes, basting occasionally.

5. Serve hot with syrup from the bottom of the skillet.

SERVE WITH: *These roasted peaches are even more delicious with a scoop of Vanilla Ice Cream (page 206) or Whipped Cream (page 212).*

# Chocolate Mousse

*This recipe is incredibly versatile! Serve it as a cool, classic, chocolate mousse and you cannot go wrong. But don't limit yourself to serving it cold. With a little warmth, this mousse softens beautifully to be used as an ice cream topping (page 206), with crèpes (page 194), or to dip truffles (page 204),! The possibilities are endless!*

---

Prep time: 7 minutes + refrigeration  ✺  Cook time: 8 minutes  ✺  Yield: 6 servings

---

## INGREDIENTS

¼ cup + 2 tablespoons (1.8 ounces) toasted carob powder

¼ cup + 2 tablespoons (2.6 ounces) coconut oil

1 cup (8½ ounces) coconut cream (see special note below)

2 tablespoons honey

Whipped Cream (page 212)

---

NOTE: *My favorite brand of toasted carob powder is Chatfield's.*

*Coconut cream can be scooped off the top of a can of full fat coconut milk, which has been refrigerated for at least 24 hours (the cream separates from the water at cold temperatures). To make sure you have enough cream for the recipe, I recommend chilling at least two cans. Save the leftover coconut water, if there is any, for a smoothie (page 216).*

---

## INSTRUCTIONS

1.  Combine first four ingredients in a saucepan. Stir over medium heat until melted, ensuring there are no lumps, about five to six minutes.

2.  Divide between six small ramekins and refrigerate for at least two hours.

3.  Serve with a generous dollop of whipped cream and fresh berries!

# Chocolate-Dipped Lemon Truffles

*This recipe makes use of the decadent Chocolate Mousse on page 202, though here you use it to coat truffles rather than eating it straight! Either way, a lot of finger licking is involved! These little truffles are the perfect indulgence to accompany an afternoon cup of tea with friends!*

Prep time: 30 minutes + refrigeration  ❧  Cook time: 6 minutes  ❧  Yield: 14 truffles

## INGREDIENTS

6 Medjool dates, pitted and roughly chopped

½ cup (1.4 ounces) unsweetened shredded coconut

⅓ cup (2.8 ounces) coconut oil, melted

2 tablespoons lemon juice

Chocolate Mousse (page 202)

Zest of one lemon, for garnish

\* Special equipment needed: blender or food processor

## INSTRUCTIONS

1. In a blender or food processor, combine dates, shredded coconut, coconut oil, and lemon juice. Mix on high until you obtain a smooth paste, about 15 seconds.

2. Refrigerate for two hours or until paste is firm.

3. Once firm, use a tablespoon to form paste into half balls. Place truffles onto a plate and refrigerate.

4. Prepare chocolate mousse.

5. When mousse is ready, allow to cool and thicken slightly. Working with one truffle at a time, dip truffles into mousse and place on a wire rack or parchment-lined baking sheet.

6. Sprinkle immediately with lemon zest and refrigerate for at least one hour before serving.

7. Truffles are best served chilled..

NOTE: *Will keep in the refrigerator up to 5 days.*

# Vanilla Ice Cream

*A timeless classic that can be served on its own or as an accompaniment to many desserts, such as French Crêpes (page 194), Chocolate Mousse (page 202), Honey-Lavender Roasted Peaches (page 200), or my Signature Pear Cake (page 198)! With only three ingredients, it is quite simple and straightforward. I like this vanilla ice cream best immediately after churning. Why wait?*

Prep time: 5 minutes + churning time ❧ Cook time: 5 minutes ❧ Yield: 3½ cups

## INGREDIENTS

*2 cans (13½ ounces each) full fat coconut milk*

*4 tablespoons maple syrup*

*½ teaspoon vanilla powder*

*\* Special equipment needed: ice cream maker*

## INSTRUCTIONS

1.  Add all ingredients to a saucepan and heat over medium-low heat for about five minutes, stirring regularly, until thoroughly combined.

2.  Check sweetness and adjust to taste.

3.  Allow liquid to cool completely. (Refrigeration will speed the process.)

4.  Pour liquid into the frozen bowl of an ice-cream maker and churn, following the manufacturer's instructions.

5.  Enjoy immediately as soft serve or freeze for at least one hour before serving as ice cream.

NOTE: *When frozen solid, allow ice cream to soften at room temperature for about 20 minutes before serving.*

# Citrus Ice Cream

*Citrus is one of my favorite flavors, especially in desserts and treats! I find it so refreshing and invigorating. This citrus ice cream is no exception.*

Prep time: 10 minutes + churning time ⁊ Cook time: 5 minutes ⁊ Yield: 3½ cups

## INGREDIENTS

*2 ¼ cups (19 ounces) full fat coconut milk*

*Zest of one orange*

*Zest of one lemon*

*Juice of two oranges*

*Juice of two lemons*

*3 tablespoons honey*

*\* Special equipment needed: ice cream maker*

## INSTRUCTIONS

1.  Combine all ingredients in a saucepan and stir over medium–low heat for about five minutes.

2.  Check sweetness and adjust to taste.

3.  Allow liquid to cool completely. (Refrigeration will speed the process.)

4.  Once cooled, pour liquid into the frozen bowl of an ice-cream maker and churn, following the manufacturer's instructions.

5.  Enjoy immediately as soft serve or freeze for at least an hour before serving as ice cream.

NOTE: *When frozen solid, allow ice cream to soften at room temperature for about 20 minutes before serving.*

# Afternoon Tea Time Cookies

*These scrumptious cookies are a huge hit at my house, not only with the kids, but also with my husband. They remind me of the cinnamon thins and snickerdoodles of my youth. They are light, decidedly crunchy, and very addictive!*

Prep time: 10 minutes  ❧  Cook time: 12 minutes  ❧  Yield: 2 dozen cookies

## INGREDIENTS

### ❧ CINNAMON VERSION

1 cup (3 ½ ounces) tigernut flour

¾ cup (3.3 ounces) arrowroot flour

1 teaspoon baking soda

1 teaspoon ground cinnamon

¼ teaspoon fine sea salt

½ cup (3.2 ounces) palm shortening, melted

¼ cup (3 ounces) maple syrup

1 tablespoon gelatin powder

### ❧ CAROB VERSION

1 cup (3 ½ ounces) tigernut flour

¾ cup (3.3 ounces) arrowroot flour

4 teaspoons toasted carob powder

1 teaspoon baking soda

1 teaspoon ground cinnamon

¼ teaspoon fine sea salt

½ cup + 1 tablespoon (3.6 ounces) palm shortening, melted

¼ cup + 1 tablespoon (3.7 ounces) maple syrup

1 tablespoon gelatin powder

## INSTRUCTIONS

1. Heat oven to 350° F. Place the rack in the top third of the oven. Line two baking sheets with parchment paper.

2. In a large bowl, combine tigernut flour, arrowroot flour, carob powder (if making carob version), baking soda, cinnamon, and sea salt.

3. In a small dish, mix melted palm shortening with maple syrup. Sprinkle gelatin powder over liquid and whisk vigorously for a few seconds until frothy, ensuring there are no lumps.

4. Pour liquid over dry ingredients and mix well with a spatula until a soft dough forms.

5. Scoop out small portions of dough with a tablespoon. Using your hands, roll dough into small balls, then flatten into a cookie shape. Place onto the lined baking sheets.

6. Repeat until the baking sheet is full. Cookies will spread just a little while baking.

7. Bake until cookies are lightly browned around the edges, about 12 minutes. Remove from the baking sheet immediately and allow to cool on a wire rack.

NOTE: *Store cookies in an airtight container.*

# hipped Cream

*A delicious, creamy treat to top off almost any dessert!*

Prep time: 5 minutes + refrigeration ❧ Cook time: n/a ❧ Yield: 1½ cups

## INGREDIENTS

*1 cup (8½ ounces) coconut cream
(see special note below)*

*½ tablespoon honey*

*\* Special equipment needed: hand mixer*

## INSTRUCTIONS

1. In a tall, narrow container, add coconut cream and honey. Using a hand mixer, beat cream on high until smooth, about one minute. Check sweetness and adjust to taste. Beat for another 30 seconds if you add more honey.

2. Cover and chill in the refrigerator for at least four hours for a firm whipped cream.

# Raspberry Whipped Cream

Prep time: 10 minutes + refrigeration ❧ Cook time: n/a ❧ Yield: 1⅓ cups

## INGREDIENTS

*¾ cup (3 ounces) fresh raspberries*

*½ tablespoon honey*

*1 cup (8½ ounces) coconut cream
(see special note below)*

*\* Special equipment needed: immersion
blender and hand mixer*

## INSTRUCTIONS

1. Place raspberries and honey in a tall, narrow container and purée with an immersion blender.

2. Add coconut cream. Using a hand mixer, beat cream on high until smooth, about one minute. Check sweetness and adjust to taste. Beat for another 30 seconds if you add more honey.

3. Cover and chill in the refrigerator for at least four hours for a firm whipped cream.

NOTE: *Coconut cream can be scooped off the top of a can of full fat coconut milk, which has been refrigerated for at least 24 hours (the cream separates from the water at cold temperatures). To make sure you have enough cream for the recipe, I recommend chilling at least two cans. Save the leftover coconut water, if there is any, for a smoothie (page 216).*

# Triple Berry Sauce

*This berry sauce is quite versatile. Serve warm or cold with French Crêpes (page 194), over Vanilla Ice-Cream (page 206), or with anything and everything you fancy! It is also quite delicious on its own as a light dessert after a more substantial meal.*

Prep time: 5 minutes  ✿  Cook time: 20 minutes  ✿  Yield: 1½ cups

## INGREDIENTS

1 cup (5 ounces) fresh blueberries

1 cup (5 ounces) fresh strawberries, chopped

1 cup (4 ounces) fresh raspberries

¼ cup (2 ounces) water

½ tablespoon honey

## INSTRUCTIONS

1. Combine all ingredients in a saucepan and bring to a low simmer over medium heat.

2. Cook, stirring occasionally, until fruit is tender and sauce has thickened a little, about 20 minutes.

3. Serve warm or cold, alone or accompanied, as desired.

NOTE: *Will keep in the refrigerator up to 5 days.*

# Blackberry and Pear Smoothie

*Fruit smoothies are a treat I never tire of. Try these new flavor combos to start your day or as an afternoon pick-me-up!*

Prep time: 5 minutes  ❧  Cook time: n/a  ❧  Yield: 2 cups

## INGREDIENTS

1 ½ cups (6 ounces) frozen blackberries

1 pear, peeled and roughly chopped

1 cup (8 ½ ounces) coconut water, chilled

\* Special equipment needed: blender

## INSTRUCTIONS

1. Combine all ingredients in a blender and mix until smooth.

2. Serve immediately.

NOTE: *Optional extras for your smoothie: coconut milk for creaminess, collagen powder for protein, ice cubes for crunch.*

# Peach and Cantaloupe Smoothie

Prep time: 10 minutes  ❧  Cook time: n/a  ❧  Yield: 2 cups

## INGREDIENTS

1 ½ cups (6 ounces) frozen peaches, roughly chopped

1 cup (5 ounces) chopped cantaloupe

1 cup (8 ½ ounces) coconut water, chilled

\* Special equipment needed: blender

## INSTRUCTIONS

1. Combine all ingredients in a blender and mix until smooth.

2. Serve immediately.

NOTE: *Optional extras for your smoothie: coconut milk for creaminess, collagen powder for protein, ice cubes for crunch.*

# Gingerade

*This gingerade really packs a punch and is incredibly refreshing! It is very popular with my children. Peeling the fresh ginger is a little time consuming, but the end result is really worth it.*

Prep time: 10 minutes + refrigeration  ℘  Cook time: n/a  ℘  Yield: 1½ quarts

## INGREDIENTS

*1 cup (8½ ounces) lemon juice*

*½ cup (6 ounces) honey*

*⅓ cup (1.3 ounces) peeled and roughly chopped fresh ginger*

*1 quart water*

*\* Special equipment needed: blender*

## INSTRUCTIONS

1. Combine lemon, honey, and ginger in a blender. Blend until smooth.

2. Transfer lemon mixture to a large pitcher and add water.

3. Refrigerate for at least an hour and serve chilled with ice-cubes.

# Lavender-Rose Tea Blend

*A distinctive and fragrant tea blend to enjoy any time of the day.*

Prep time: 5 minutes ❧ Cook time: 4 minutes ❧ Yield: 1½ cups

## INGREDIENTS

*1 cup (1.2 ounces) whole rose buds*

*½ cup (2.8 ounces) jasmine green tea
(see special note below)*

*1 teaspoon dried lavender flowers*

*Honey, optional*

*Lemon, optional*

## INSTRUCTIONS

1. Combine rose buds, green tea, and lavender in an airtight container. Tea blend can be stored at room temperature until ready to use.

2. To prepare tea: brew one tablespoon tea with eight ounces water at just under boiling point for two to four minutes. Adjust brew strength to suit your taste.

3. Strain into a teacup and enjoy as is or garnished with honey or lemon, or both!

NOTE: *Green tea is allowed on the Paleo Autoimmune Protocol, but should be consumed in moderation. White tea may be substituted.*

No. 8

BASICS

# Mint and Basil Pesto

*I grow basil and mint in my kitchen garden every year so that I always have fresh herbs on hand to prepare this pesto. You don't need a lot of space to grow your own herbs; a few planters and a bag of dirt will transform your little balcony into an urban garden! Serve this pesto with Bacon Wrapped Asparagus (page 70) or pretty much any thing else!*

Prep time: 15 minutes 🍃 Cook time: n/a 🍃 Yield: ½ cup

## INGREDIENTS

*2 cups chopped fresh basil leaves*

*2 cups mint leaves*

*2 cloves garlic, minced*

*¼ cup + 2 tablespoons extra-virgin olive oil*

*2 teaspoons lemon juice*

*Pinch fine sea salt*

*\* Special equipment needed: blender or food processor*

## INSTRUCTIONS

1. Combine all ingredients in a blender or food processor. Mix on medium speed for 30 seconds or until pesto reaches your preferred consistency.

2. You may have to stop once or twice to scrape down the sides of the blender or food processor with a spatula.

3. Transfer pesto to an airtight container and refrigerate until needed.

NOTE: *Will keep in the refrigerator up to 5 days.*

SERVE WITH: *Bacon Wrapped Asparagus (page 70), Grilled Lamb Chops (page 164), No Nightshade Ratatouille (page 128), or Rainbow Chard, Beef, and Cauliflower Soup (page 124).*

# Chunky Black Olive Tapenade

*Tapenade is traditionally made with black olives that have completely ripened on the tree and lost much of their bitterness. I prefer mine lightly processed, with little bits of olives and garlic peeking through. This tapenade is delicious served with my Crisp Oregano Crackers (page 230) or simply on slices of green apple. It is also a delicious accompaniment to roast lamb, pork, poultry, or fish.*

Prep time: 8 minutes ❧ Cook time: n/a ❧ Yield: 1 cup

## INGREDIENTS

*1 cup black olives, pitted*

*2 tablespoons capers*

*2 cloves garlic, minced*

*1 teaspoon chopped fresh rosemary*

*½ teaspoon Herbes de Provence (page 232)*

*\* Special equipment needed: blender or food processor*

## INSTRUCTIONS

1. Combine all ingredients in a blender or food processor. Mix on low for 10 seconds.

2. Take care not to overmix; tapenade will taste better if left a little "chunky."

3. Transfer to an airtight container and refrigerate until needed.

NOTE: *Will keep in the refrigerator up to 7 days.*

SERVE WITH: *Baked Cod (page 174), Oven-Roasted Fennel and Garlic (page 130), Roasted Vegetable Medley (page 134), Sage Roast Chicken (page 150), Herbed Roast Lamb (page 152), or Oven-Baked Snapper with Fennel (page 184).*

# Nomato Sauce

*No nightshades? No problem! If you thought that the Paleo Autoimmune Protocol was hard, think again! This vibrant Nomato sauce will make you forget about tomatoes and peppers. Apply liberally to anything and everything you wish, but especially my Meatballs (page 168).*

Prep time: 6 minutes ❧ Cook time: n/a ❧ Yield: 2 cups

## INGREDIENTS

*1 can (15-ounce) butternut squash purée (about 1½ cups)*

*2 medium cooked beets (about ½ pound), roughly chopped*

*1½ teaspoons apple cider vinegar*

*1½ teaspoons coconut aminos*

*1 teaspoon dried basil*

*1 teaspoon dried marjoram*

*1 teaspoon fine sea salt*

*\* Special equipment needed: blender or food processor*

## INSTRUCTIONS

1. Combine all ingredients in a blender or food processor. Mix until smooth and creamy, about 20 seconds. Check seasoning and adjust salt to taste.

2. Store in a glass container in the refrigerator and warm as needed before serving.

NOTE: *Will keep in the refrigerator up to 5 days.*

SERVE WITH: *No Nightshade Ratatouille (page 128), Balsamic Spaghetti Squash (page 136), Herbed Roast Lamb (page 152), Rustic Beef and Pork Meatloaf (page 160), or Meatballs (page 168).*

# Crisp Oregano Crackers

*These crackers are deliciously crispy and packed with flavor. Feel free to experiment with your favorite dried herbs.*

Prep time: 5 minutes ❧ Cook time: 12 minutes ❧ Yield: 25 crackers

## INGREDIENTS

½ cup (2 ounces) tigernut flour

½ cup (2.6 ounces) cassava flour

3 teaspoons dried oregano

½ teaspoon fine sea salt

½ cup (4.2 ounces) water

2 tablespoons extra-virgin olive oil

---

NOTE: *Store crackers in an airtight container to preserve their crispness.*

---

SERVE WITH: *Rillettes (page 62), Creamy Liver Pâté (page 66), or Chunky Black Olive Tapenade (page 226).*

## INSTRUCTIONS

1. Heat oven to 400° F. Set the rack in the top third of the oven. Line two baking sheets with parchment paper.

2. In a large bowl, combine all dry ingredients and mix well. Add water and olive oil. Using a wooden spoon, mix until a soft dough forms.

3. Using your hands, roll half tablespoons of dough into balls. Place onto the baking sheet and flatten with your fingers. If dough is too sticky to flatten easily, simply place a small piece of parchment paper on top while you press down with your fingers.

4. Bake crackers until edges start to turn brown, about 11 to 12 minutes.

5. If you want a super crunchy cracker, bake one minute longer.

# Herbes de Provence

*Herbes de Provence are widely used in French cuisine. It is a wonderful seasoning blend for many dishes, including grilled and roasted meat, fish, and vegetables. This version is my staple herb mix, but I encourage you to experiment with the blend that most appeals to you! You can easily make your own to keep and use as needed.*

Prep time: 5 minutes  ᔕ  Cook time: n/a  ᔕ  Yield: ½ cup

## INGREDIENTS

2 tablespoons dried basil

2 tablespoons dried marjoram

2 tablespoons dried rosemary

2 tablespoons dried thyme

½ teaspoon dried lavender flowers

## INSTRUCTIONS

1. Blend spices together and store in an airtight container until needed.

2. Crush with a mortar and pestle if a finer consistency is desired.

NOTE: *This mix also makes a beautiful hostess gift when put into a pretty jar with a ribbon!*

*If you are able to collect your own herbs and dry them, the final result will be even better. Hang small bundles of the herbs upside down in a cool, dry place. When the bundles are dry, crumble them between your hands and store as above. You may process the herbs in small batches in a food processor for a finer consistency, but this is optional.*

SERVE WITH: *Marinated Olives (page 72), Roasted Vegetable Medley (page 134), or Lavender and Honey Pork Medallions (page 166).*

# Simple Chicken Bone Broth

*Bone broth is one of the essentials of a healing diet. It is incredibly nutrient-dense, rich in beneficial gelatin, and so good for gut health. You can drink it on its own or as a base for numerous soups and sauces. Feel free to experiment with whatever bones you have on hand and with your favorite herbs and spices. The key here is a long slow cook to extract all the goodness from the bones.*

Prep time: 5 minutes  ❧  Cook time: 8 hours +  ❧  Yield: 3 quarts

## INGREDIENTS

*2 ½ to 3 pounds chicken bones*

*1 sprig rosemary (optional)*

*3 quarts water*

*1 tablespoon apple cider vinegar*

*\* Special equipment needed: 6-quart slow cooker*

## INSTRUCTIONS

1. Place all ingredients into a slow cooker. Cover with water. Secure lid and simmer for at least eight hours and up to 24 hours.

2. When broth is done, discard bones and strain liquid into airtight glass containers.

3. Store in the refrigerator or freezer until needed.

NOTE: *Will keep in the refrigerator up to 7 days.*

# Fish Bone Broth

As with Chicken Bone Broth (page 234), fish bone broth is an essential part of the Paleo Autoimmune Protocol for its nutritional value. It is a potent defense, albeit often unknown, against illness and inflammation. Plus, a good homemade fish broth tastes so much better than what you could ever buy in a store! Use it as a base for delicious seafood preparations and soups.

Prep time: 10 minutes  ∾  Cook time: 8 hours  ∾  Yield: 2½ quarts

## INGREDIENTS

2½ to 3 pounds mixed fish bones

1 medium yellow onion, quartered

1 large carrot, cut in half lengthwise and roughly chopped

1 leek, washed, cut in half lengthwise and roughly chopped

4 sprigs fresh thyme

1 bay leaf

1 tablespoon apple cider vinegar

2½ quarts water

\* Special equipment needed: 6-quart slow cooker

## INSTRUCTIONS

1. Place all ingredients in a slow cooker. Cover with water. Secure lid and simmer for eight hours.

2. When broth is done, strain liquid into airtight glass containers, discarding all bones, vegetables, and herbs.

3. Store in the refrigerator or freezer until needed.

NOTE: Oily fish, such as salmon, mackerel, and sardines, are not recommended when making fish bone broth. Will keep in the refrigerator up to 7 days.

# Basic Mayonnaise

*I promise you will love this rich, creamy AIP mayonnaise even if you weren't a mayo lover before! Use it liberally on salads, "sandwiches," or as a dip for fresh vegetables. Add an avocado for a lighter, greener version.*

Prep time: 5 minutes ✌ Cook time: n/a ✌ Yield: 1 cup

## INGREDIENTS

⅓ cup avocado oil

⅓ cup extra-virgin olive oil

⅓ cup palm shortening

1 teaspoon lemon juice

Pinch fine sea salt

\* Special equipment needed: blender or hand mixer

## INSTRUCTIONS

1. Combine all ingredients in a mixing bowl and beat with a hand mixer until you obtain a smooth and creamy texture. (You can also do this with a blender.) Check seasoning and adjust salt to taste.

2. Store in an airtight glass container in the refrigerator. For a creamier consistency, remove from the refrigerator about 20 minutes before serving.

NOTE: *Will keep in the refrigerator up to 7 days.*

---

# Avocado Mayonnaise

Prep time: 5 minutes ✌ Cook time: n/a ✌ Yield: 1 cup

## INGREDIENTS

1 large avocado, peeled, pitted, and chopped

¼ cup coconut milk

¼ cup palm shortening

2 teaspoons lemon juice

Pinch fine sea salt

\* Special equipment needed: blender or food processor

## INSTRUCTIONS

1. Combine all ingredients in a blender or food processor. Mix until smooth and creamy, about 20 seconds.

2. Store in an airtight glass container in the refrigerator. For a creamier consistency, remove from the refrigerator about 20 minutes before serving.

NOTE: *Will keep in the refrigerator up to 3 days.*

# Aïoli (Garlic Mayonnaise)

*Choose fresh, crisp garlic cloves with no sprout or germ. If you don't have fresh garlic on hand, you may substitute garlic powder.*

Prep time: 5 minutes ❧ Cook time: n/a ❧ Yield: ¾ cup

## INGREDIENTS

⅓ cup avocado oil

½ cup palm shortening

3 cloves garlic, minced, or ½ teaspoon garlic powder

1 tablespoon lemon juice

¼ teaspoon fine sea salt

\* Special equipment needed: immersion blender or food processor

## INSTRUCTIONS

1. Combine all ingredients in a tall, narrow container and mix thoroughly with an immersion blender. (You can also do this in a food processor.) Check seasoning and adjust salt to taste.

2. Store in an airtight glass container in the refrigerator. For a creamier consistency, remove from the refrigerator 20 minutes before serving.

NOTE: *Will keep in the refrigerator, sealed in an airtight container, up to 7 days.*

SERVE WITH: *Niçoise Salad (page 84), Shrimp and Citrus Salad (page 92), Grilled Shrimp (page 178), or Bouillabaisse-Inspired Seafood Stew (page 190).*

# Remoulade

*Remoulade is a French culinary word that is used both to describe the entire dish as well as the sauce. I know, it is confusing! Originally, it was a rich sauce made with eggs. Here is my own AIP-friendly version. It also works well as a zingy alternative to mayonnaise.*

Prep time: 5 minutes + refrigeration ❧ Cook time: 8 minutes ❧ Yield: 1¼ cups

## INGREDIENTS

⅓ cup + ½ cup Chicken Bone Broth (page 234)

2 tablespoons arrowroot flour

½ cup full fat coconut milk

3 teaspoons lemon juice

½ teaspoon fine sea salt

## INSTRUCTIONS

1. In a small bowl, combine ⅓ cup chicken broth with arrowroot flour and stir until powder is thoroughly dissolved. Set aside.

2. In a saucepan, combine ½ cup chicken broth, coconut milk, lemon juice, and sea salt. Mix well and bring to a low boil.

3. Pour arrowroot mixture into boiling sauce and stir until sauce thickens, about 20 to 30 seconds.

4. Check seasoning and adjust salt to taste. (Keep in mind that food served cold needs more salt.)

5. Transfer to a glass container and refrigerate for two to three hours or until thoroughly chilled.

NOTE: *Will keep in the refrigerator up to 7 days.*

SERVE WITH: *Celeriac Remoulade (page 138), Pork Shoulder Picnic Roast (page 162), or Oven Baked Snapper with Fennel (page 184).*

# Basic Vinaigrette

Prep time: 5 minutes ❧ Cook time: n/a ❧ Yield: 1 cup

### INGREDIENTS

⅔ cup extra-virgin olive oil

⅓ cup apple cider vinegar

½ teaspoon fine sea salt

### INSTRUCTIONS

1. Combine all ingredients in a jar with a tight fitting lid.

2. Shake well before each use. Keep at room temperature.

# Shallot Vinaigrette

Prep time: 10 minutes ❧ Cook time: n/a ❧ Yield: 1½ cups

### INGREDIENTS

1 cup extra-virgin olive oil

⅓ cup apple cider vinegar

1 tablespoon honey

¼ cup minced shallots

¼ cup minced chives

### INSTRUCTIONS

1. Add all ingredients to a glass jar with a secure lid. Shake to combine.

2. Store in the refrigerator until needed. Shake well before use. Will keep in the refrigerator up to 7 days.

# Strawberry Vinaigrette

Prep time: 10 minutes ❧ Cook time: n/a ❧ Yield: ¾ cup

### INGREDIENTS

1 cup strawberries, stemmed and quartered

2 tablespoons extra-virgin olive oil

1 tablespoon balsamic vinegar

½ tablespoon lemon juice

¼ teaspoon fine sea salt

### INSTRUCTIONS

1. Combine all ingredients in a blender or food processor. Mix until smooth and creamy, about 20 seconds.

2. Store in the refrigerator until needed. Shake well before use. Will keep in the refrigerator up to 7 days.

# RECIPE INDEX

# INDEX OF INGREDIENTS